COMPLETE CONDITIONING FOR VOLLEYBALL

Steve Oldenburg

Human Kinetics

Library of Congress Cataloging-in-Publication Data

Oldenburg, Steve.
 Complete conditioning for volleyball / Steve Oldenburg.
     pages cm.
1. Volleyball--Training. 2. Volleyball--Coaching. I. Title.
 GV1015.5.T73O54 2015
 796.325--dc23

2014011684

ISBN: 978-1-4504-5971-6 (print)

This publication is written and published to provide accurate and authoritative information relevant to the subject matter presented. It is published and sold with the understanding that the author and publisher are not engaged in rendering legal, medical, or other professional services by reason of their authorship or publication of this work. If medical or other expert assistance is required, the services of a competent professional person should be sought.

The web addresses cited in this text were current as of May 2014, unless otherwise noted.

Acquisitions Editor: Justin Klug; **Developmental Editor:** Cynthia McEntire; **Managing Editor:** Elizabeth Evans; **Copyeditor:** Patsy Fortney; **Permissions Manager:** Martha Gullo; **Graphic Designer:** Julie L. Denzer; **Cover Designer:** Keith Blomberg; **Photograph (cover):** Craig Pessman; **Photographs (interior):** © Human Kinetics; **Video Producer:** Doug Fink; **Video Production Coordinator:** Amy Rose; **Photo Production Manager**: Jason Allen; **Art Manager:** Kelly Hendren; **Associate Art Manager:** Alan L. Wilborn; **Illustrations:** © Human Kinetics; **Printer:** Sheridan Books

We thank the University of Illinois at Urbana–Champaign for assistance in providing the location for the photo shoot for this book.

Human Kinetics books are available at special discounts for bulk purchase. Special editions or book excerpts can also be created to specification. For details, contact the Special Sales Manager at Human Kinetics. The video contents of this product are licensed for private home use and traditional, face-to-face classroom instruction only. For public performance licensing, please contact a sales representative at www. HumanKinetics.com/SalesRepresentatives.

Printed in the United States of America   10 9 8 7 6 5 4 3 2 1

The paper in this book is certified under a sustainable forestry program.

Human Kinetics
Website: www.HumanKinetics.com

United States: Human Kinetics
P.O. Box 5076
Champaign, IL 61825-5076
800-747-4457
e-mail: humank@hkusa.com

Canada: Human Kinetics
475 Devonshire Road Unit 100
Windsor, ON N8Y 2L5
800-465-7301 (in Canada only)
e-mail: info@hkcanada.com

Europe: Human Kinetics
107 Bradford Road
Stanningley
Leeds LS28 6AT, United Kingdom
+44 (0) 113 255 5665
e-mail: hk@hkeurope.com

Australia: Human Kinetics
57A Price Avenue
Lower Mitcham, South Australia 5062
08 8372 0999
e-mail: info@hkaustralia.com

New Zealand: Human Kinetics
P.O. Box 80
Torrens Park, South Australia 5062
0800 222 062
e-mail: info@hknewzealand.com

E6000

COMPLETE CONDITIONING FOR VOLLEYBALL

Contents

Video Contents

Mobility

Three-Plane Ankle Mob
Shoulder Flexion Mob
Hand Walkout With Three-Plane
Reach
Spiderman Crawl
Forearm to Instep Complex

Balance and Stability

Matrix Reaches
Single-Leg Squat
Single-Arm, Single-Leg Deadlift
Single-Leg Deadlift
Walking Lunge With Medicine
Ball Arc

Strength

Back Squat
Front Squat
Box Step-Up
Bent Row
Supine Row

Power

Hang Snatch
Power Snatch
VertiMax Pause, Jump, Squat
VertiMax Jump Squat Singles
Lateral Hop, Hop, Bound
Forward Hop, Hop, Bound
Forward Hop, Hop, Lateral Bound
Back Hop, Hop, Lateral Bound

Quickness and Agility

Lateral Three-Line Agility
Forward-and-Back Three-Line
Agility
Backpedal Intervals
Pivot Sprint
Forward Sprint to Pivot Sprint
Single-Plane Mirror Drill
Cross Mirror Drill

Core Training and Shoulder Prehab

Supine Lateral Ball Roll
Slide Board Mountain Climber
Multidirection Weight Plate
Shoulder Press
Medicine Ball Chop Toss
Overhead Medicine Ball Crunch
Toss
Overhead Medicine Ball Oblique
Toss

Conditioning

Timed Shuffle
Jump, Shuffle, Jump, Sprint
Conditioning
Position Threes

Dynamic Warm-Up

Forward Plyo Skip
Backward Plyo Skip
Lateral Plyo Skip

Accessing
the Online Video

This book includes access to online video that includes 42 clips demonstrating some of the most dynamic exercises discussed in the book. Throughout the book, exercises marked with this play button icon indicate where the content is enhanced by online video clips: ▶

Take the following steps to access the video. If you need help at any point in the process, you can contact us by clicking on the Technical Support link under Customer Service on the right side of the screen.

1. Visit www.HumanKinetics.com/CompleteConditioningforVolleyball.
2. Click on the **View online video** link next to the book cover.
3. You will be directed to the screen shown in figure 1. Click the **Sign In** link on the left or top of the page. If you do not have an account with Human Kinetics, you will be prompted to create one.

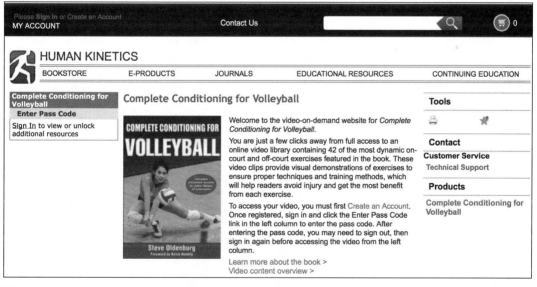

Figure 1

4. If the online video does not appear in the list on the left of the page, click the **Enter Pass Code** option in that list. Enter the pass code exactly as it is printed here, including all hyphens. Click the Submit button to unlock the online video. After you have entered this pass code the first time, you will never have to enter

it again. For future visits, all you need to do is sign in to the book's website and follow the link that appears in the left menu.

Pass code for online video: Oldenburg-8W3RM-OLV

5. Once you have signed into the site and entered the pass code, select **Online Video** from the list on the left side of the screen. You'll then see an Online Video page with information about the video, as shown in the screenshot in figure 2. You can go straight to the accompanying videos for each topic by clicking on the blue links at the bottom of the page.

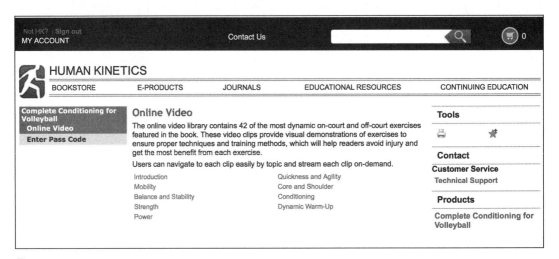

Figure 2

6. You are now able to view video for the topic you selected on the previous screen, as well as all others that accompany this product. Across the top of the page, you will see a set of buttons that correspond to the topics in the text that have accompanying video, as shown in figure 3. Once you click on a topic, a player will appear. In the player, the clips for that topic will appear vertically along the right side. Select the video you would like to watch and view it in the

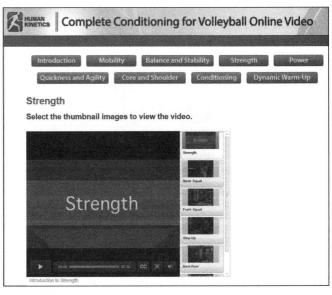

Figure 3

main player window. You can use the buttons at the bottom of the main player window to view the video full screen, to turn captioning on and off, and to pause, fast-forward, or reverse the clip.

Foreword

One of the frustrations that many volleyball coaches deal with is finding strength and conditioning coaches who understand volleyball. Strength and conditioning coaches have typically come from football, and many hope to work in football in the future. So the frustration comes from the fact that volleyball players are in strength development programs designed to make great football players, and it has nothing to do with volleyball. Many athletes are trained to gain mass and push a lot of weight. The strength coaches they come in contact with might know nothing about volleyball and don't understand the demands on the bodies or the number of jumps that are required in the sport.

Volleyball coaches understand the importance of strength and conditioning, but that doesn't mean they know *how* to train their team. They might know exercises that can help, but they don't understand the techniques or the periodization required for getting the most out of their athletes or making the best use of their time. Most coaches have never been trained and do not have the science background to understand what is required.

This book addresses those frustrations. Steve Oldenburg started working with the Illinois volleyball program in 2006. Before that, we had athletes who were lacking in explosion and had a lot of injuries to their lower legs. The players were very strong in their upper bodies but also very inflexible. Since that time they have fewer injuries, they are long and lean, they are jumping higher, and, most important, they are trained individually based on positions. Steve gets what it means to be a volleyball player and knows how to train the athletes so that they can maximize their athletic ability.

What I love about working with Steve is that he is always searching, always questioning how we can be better. Steve started his career as a rehab specialist. As a result, he became familiar with training stability and flexibility in joints. He brings this expertise to a sport that involves dynamic jumping and landing along with contorted body positions required for gaining control of the ball. Steve's expertise is one of the main reasons for our decrease in injuries.

In this book not only will you have a plan to train your team, but you will also learn about how the body moves and how to get your team ready for the season. It has worked tremendously for us, and I know it will for you, too.

Kevin Hambly, Head Women's Volleyball Coach,
University of Illinois

Introduction

Volleyball is an amazing sport. On many levels, it is played offensively by explosive, high-flying athletes with cannons for arms, and defensively by athletes with quick, split-second reactions and at times digging balls in acrobat-like positions. To be successful at the highest level, volleyball athletes must be mobile, stable, strong, powerful, and quick. *Complete Conditioning for Volleyball* describes in detail the process for developing explosive, injury-resistant athletes specific to this sport. This approach uses a multilayered system in which each layer builds on the previous one to promote continued success in each session, cycle, and year as well as throughout an athlete's career.

Before this journey begins, we first take a look at where we are now. Part I, Individual Assessment and Testing, explains how to create athlete profiles. Chapter 1 outlines a systematic process to assess, evaluate, and implement corrective measures for posture, basic movement efficiency, and length-tension testing. Uncovering and correcting mobility and stability issues should be the strength and conditioning coach's primary concern. If any of these issues are left unresolved, no matter how well designed and well implemented the training program is, gains will be minimal and eventually plateau. Chapter 2 presents specific tests and processes of data collection. These numbers are important not only because they serve to motivate the athlete, but also because they allow the strength and conditioning coach to track athlete progress, compare individuals, and manipulate loading parameters from session to session as well as within a session for any given exercise.

Part II presents the meat and potatoes of the program, the six components of training: mobility, stability, strength, power, quickness, and conditioning. It also includes a chapter on core training and shoulder prehabilitation. Chapter 3, Mobility, and chapter 4, Balance and Stability, are the foundations for training. Without these two components an athlete will never optimize her strength, power, or quickness. The ability to create efficient angles and move fluidly through space are essential for making plays on the court as well as for achieving proper range of motion (ROM) and technique in many exercises in the weight room. For example, if an athlete has a severe restriction in ankle dorsiflexion, the easiest way to make her quicker is to make the joint more mobile. This is discussed in chapter 3. If the small muscles that stabilize joints are not firing, are firing incorrectly, or are weak, the bigger muscles such as the glutes, hamstrings, and quads will not be able to maximize their force production. Chapter 4 discusses the importance of balance and stability and presents exercises to maximize both throughout the body. Chapter 5, Strength, dives into the importance of force production to achieve a volleyball athlete's ultimate goals: to jump higher and move quicker.

Once athletes are more mobile, more stable, stronger (i.e., can generate force), it's time to work on moving some weight or their bodies fast. Chapter 6 outlines both weight room–based and plyometric-based training. It also provides exercises to improve power. Whether the athlete is accelerating out of an athletic stance, changing direction to dig a ball, or approaching to attack, quickness is essential. Chapter 7 discusses proper posture to play defense, proper mechanics to initiate movement, and ways to move efficiently. Exercises and their progressions are also presented. Chapter 8, Core Training and Shoulder Prehab, might surprise you. We discuss how the common crunch could have a negative effect on power production during an attack and the fact that the sequence of movement and preload of the core is what produces a cannon of an arm. A volleyball athlete has to be quick and explosive from the first serve to the last point of a five-set match, from week to week and throughout the competitive season.

Chapter 9 discusses how to properly ramp up off-season conditioning by developing a base, transitioning to more volleyball-specific movements, and then executing position-specific court conditioning. A proper progression of off-season conditioning is important because it allows the coach to unload the athlete and track and progress the number of floor contacts (landings from jumps) and changes of directions throughout a cycle. Also, when athletes come into the preseason with a conditioning base specific to their positions, the coaching staff can focus on strategy, the team's system of play, technique, and simply volleyball instead of spending more time on developing a base of conditioning.

It's time to bring it all together! Part III provides the plan of action. Chapter 10 dives into creating an individual mobility program based on the assessments from chapter 1 and presents a dynamic warm-up to prepare the body to train. This chapter also outlines a general mobility program you can use immediately while you are familiarizing yourself with the assessment process. Chapters 11 and 12 present off-season and in-season programs. These chapters give you a week-by-week look at how elite collegiate athletes train. The main goal of the off-season program is to lay a solid base of mobility and stability while maximizing strength, power, and quickness. Because of the high demands of match play, the in-season training program focuses on injury prevention, maintenance of strength and power, and recovery.

In the decade that I have worked with professional and collegiate athletes, one thing has always held true. No matter the sport, a sound year-round training program is the foundation for athletic development. Taking it a step further, program implementation is where the tangible results are achieved. To properly implement a program, a strength and conditioning coach must lead, teach, and create a positive environment for the athlete to be productive. Emphasis should be on discipline, hard work, dedication, and accountability. Coaches should demonstrate and give detailed descriptions of what to focus on prior to having athletes perform a new exercise or one they haven't performed in a while. They should give short cues while athletes are performing an exercise and, if necessary, elaborate only after the set is complete. Coaches should not just tell athletes what to do; they should also tell them why they should do it. When athletes know the why, they are more likely to meticulously execute the exercise or drill. Maybe the most important thing a coach can do is bring energy, enthusiasm, and a positive attitude to the gym every day. Creating an environment in which athletes are genuinely excited to be there, want to work hard, and are committed to the goal of getting better is just as important as the content of the program.

This book is also accompanied by online video clips that show how to perform some of the most dynamic exercises correctly. As the athletes in the video clips complete several reps of each exercise, you see the proper technique, helping you to fully benefit from each exercise.

The exercises that have accompanying online video are all listed in the Video Contents and are also marked with this symbol in the text: ▶

I often repeat a phrase that I hope sticks in the brains of my athletes: "Today we have an opportunity. You must decide if you are going to work or if you are going to train!" Working means going through the motions doing just what is asked of you. Training is much more. It is an obsession, a greater focus on the task at hand, an effort that transcends what you thought you were capable of. It is driven by the hunger to be better than yesterday with the knowledge that you will not be as good as tomorrow. I hope this book gives you a foundation of information about training smart as you, whether coach or athlete, create an environment that instills the hunger not just to work, but to train.

Part I

INDIVIDUAL ASSESSMENT AND TESTING

Individual assessments, performance testing, and data collection are key aspects of a sound strength and conditioning program. Assessing each athlete for postural alignment and basic movement quality helps identify mobility and stability deficits prior to beginning a training program. If marked deficits are found, an individualized plan to correct the deficits can be implemented, proper exercise progression established, and contraindicated exercises adjusted or avoided. Performance testing is a vital component to the training process because it helps determine whether the program and its implementation are successful. Data collection is used to prescribe appropriate weights for indicated intensities on core lifts, establish goals, and gauge progress. The chapters in part I address the implementation and analysis of the screening, testing, and data collection process.

Chapter 1

Individual Assessment

Before any weight is lifted or any drill is performed, each athlete should be assessed to identify misalignments in posture, find muscle imbalances, and analyze fundamental movement quality. This is achieved by screening the athletes subjectively and quantitatively using tests and movements to ensure a solid foundation for physical training and reduce the potential for injury in volleyball. If satisfactory scores are not achieved in the movement portion of the screen, the tester must systematically assess the range of motion and length tension of each joint and muscle involved in the movement. Breaking down the movement joint by joint will identify any immobilities that restricted movement in the initial screen. If an immobility is not found, the cause of the dysfunctional movement is usually lack of joint stability or faulty movement patterning.

MOVEMENT SCREEN

The movement screen is composed of 10 tests. Seven tests—overhead squat, single-leg squat, ankle dorsiflexion, stability push-up, prone scarecrow, internal shoulder rotation, and landing competency—are scored on a 5-point scale in which 5 is excellent and 1 is poor. The posture assessment, scapular dyskinesis test, and Ober's test are qualitative tests that are not scored but are critical for understanding the overall scope of the athlete's physical state. On completion of the movement screen, test scores are recorded and graphed to give athletes and coaches visual feedback of the overall results and areas needing improvement and to identify athletes who have a higher risk of injury.

Posture Assessment

Purpose

To assess joint alignment

Setup

Set up a plumb line by suspending a string with a metal weight on one end. This is used to determine vertical alignment from a given point.

Procedure

Lateral view: Position the athlete so the plumb line is at a point just anterior to the lateral malleolus (figure 1.1a). Instruct the athlete to stand in her normal posture with her hands at her sides.

Front and back view: The plumb line bisects the body in right and left halves. The athlete stands in her normal posture with her hands at her sides (figure 1.1b).

Figure 1.1   Posture assessment: *(a)* lateral view with plumb line; *(b)* front view.

Assessment

Lateral view: In ideal alignment, these points coincide with the plumb line:

- Slightly anterior to the lateral malleolus (reference point)
- Slightly anterior to the axis of the knee
- Slightly posterior to the axis of the hip joint
- Through the bodies of the lumbar spine
- Through the shoulder joint
- Through the ear canal

Front and back view: While evaluating posture in the front and back view, compare the right and left sides for asymmetries or misalignments. Consider shoulder height; scapula height, angle, and winging; hip height; knee position; and ankle and foot position.

Common Findings

Kyphosis: Excessive curve of the thoracic spine and depression of the chest; usually presents with forward shoulder posture.

Scapula: Common dysfunctions are winging of the shoulder blades or asymmetrical misalignment vertically or horizontally.

Pelvis: Normal pelvic tilt in men is 3 to 5 degrees; in women, 7 to 10 degrees.

Lumbar lordosis: Excessive curve in the lumbar spine; usually presents with anterior pelvic tilt, tight hip flexors and lumbar extensors, and weak glutes and lower abdominals.

Flat back posture: Minimal or no curve in the lumbar spine; usually presents with posterior pelvic tilt, tight hip extensors, and weak hip flexors.

Knees: Medially rotated knees put an athlete at high risk for valgus knee movements, the movement associated with ACL tears.

Pronated feet (dropped arches): Presents as minimal to no arch in the medial border of the foot. Dropped arches usually are caused by lack of activation or weakness in the muscles on the plantar side of the foot.

Importance

Ideal postural alignment promotes optimal joint stability, movement efficiency, and respiratory function, as well as proper load distribution.

Overhead Squat

Purpose

To assess total-body mobility and stability in a bilateral stance

Setup

The athlete performs the test while barefoot. The athlete's toes are on a line, feet straight forward with the insteps of both feet in vertical alignment with the outsides of the shoulders. The athlete holds a dowel rod overhead so that the upper and lower arms are at 90-degree angles.

Procedure

- The athlete presses the dowel rod maximally overhead.
- Keeping the dowel rod in the same plane, the athlete slowly descends into the deepest squat possible (figure 1.2).
- The athlete holds for 3 seconds at the bottom of the squat and returns to the starting position.
- The athlete is given a maximum of three attempts.
- If a score of 4 or 5 is not achieved (see table 1.1 for scoring criteria), the athlete repeats the test without the dowel rod, but with elbows extended and shoulders flexed at 90 degrees so the arms are parallel to the floor.

Figure 1.2   Overhead squat.

- If a score of 3 is not achieved, the athlete repeats the test without the dowel rod, but with elbows extended and shoulders flexed at 90 degrees so the arms are parallel to the floor. The athlete's feet are rotated out 15 degrees with the insides of the heels in vertical alignment with the outsides of the shoulders.

Assessment

Table 1.1 Scoring Criteria for Overhead Squat

Score	Criteria
5	Dowel rod stays in the same plane; head, chest, and shoulders stay behind knees; knees stay aligned over feet; feet remain flat and with no outturn; and upper legs reach parallel to the floor or below.
4	Slight deviation in squat position or alignment, or upper thighs are slightly above parallel to the floor.
3	No dowel rod, arms out in front. Torso angle matches or is less than shin angle, and upper leg reaches parallel to the floor or below.
2	No dowel rod, arms out in front, feet turned out. Same criteria as a score of 3.
1	Unable to achieve upper thigh parallel to the floor or torso angle greater than shin angle.

Single-Leg Squat Assessment

Purpose

To assess single-leg mobility, stability, and strength

Setup

The athlete performs the test while barefoot. The athlete stands tall in a single-leg stance on the edge of a 6-inch (15 cm) box. The athlete flexes the arms to 90 degrees at the shoulder and holds the non-weight-bearing leg out in front of him.

Procedure

- Keeping the head up, chest out, foot flat, and hip, knee, and ankle in alignment, the athlete descends into the deepest squat possible (figure 1.3).
- The athlete holds for 2 or 3 seconds and returns to the starting position.
- The athlete performs three repetitions on each leg.

Figure 1.3 Single-leg squat assessment.

Assessment

This test is scored on two criteria: the depth of the squat (mobility; table 1.2) and balance (stability; table 1.3). Each repetition is scored independently for mobility and stability, and an average is calculated. The final depth and stability scores are averaged to get a final score.

Table 1.2 Scoring Criteria for Single-Leg Squat Depth

Score	Criteria
5	Thigh parallel to floor or below with torso angle equal to or less than shin angle.
4	Thigh just above parallel to floor or slightly greater torso-to-shin angle.
3	Thigh and shin angle of 90 degrees (half squat) with torso angle equal to or less than shin angle.
2	Thigh and shin angle of 100 to 120 degrees (quarter squat) with torso angle equal to or less than shin angle.
1	Can't achieve squat with thigh and shin angle of 120 degrees (quarter squat).

Table 1.3 Scoring Criteria for Single-Leg Squat Stability

Score	Criteria
5	Foot remains flat and aligned with knee and hip; shoulders remain centered over hips.
4	Slight deviations of foot, knee, hip, or torso.
3	Moderate deviations of foot, knee, hip, or torso.
2	Gross deviations of foot, knee, hip, or torso.
1	Unable to maintain balance on one leg.

Ankle Dorsiflexion

Purpose

To assess closed-chain ankle dorsiflexion

Setup

The tester places a piece of tape on the floor against and perpendicular to a wall. A second piece of tape is placed vertically up the wall in line with the tape on the floor. Starting at the wall, the tester draws lines on the tape on the floor at 1.5-centimeter (around 0.5 in.) increments up to 15 centimeters (6 in.).

Procedure

- The athlete faces the wall and places the longest toe of the foot being tested on the 9-centimeter (3.5 in.) line.
- The tester kneels beside the athlete, placing the tips of his three middle fingers under the arch of the athlete's foot. With the other hand, the tester grasps the athlete's heel with his thumb and index fingers. This allows the tester to feel whether the athlete's arch is caving in and feel any loss of pressure or lift of the heel.
- The athlete dorsiflexes the ankle, moving the knee to the wall while keeping the heel flat, the kneecap in line with the center toe, and the hips square to the wall (figure 1.4).
- If the athlete touches the wall, she moves her foot back to the next line and repeats the test. This process is continued until she is unable to touch the wall without lifting her heel or collapsing the arch of her foot.

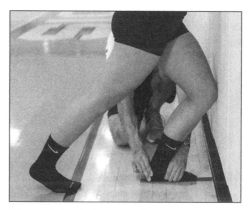

- If the athlete is unable to touch the wall at the first distance, she is instructed to move her foot forward to the next line and repeat the test. The athlete continues to move closer to the wall until she can touch her knee to the wall and all criteria are met. See table 1.4 for scores.

Figure 1.4   Ankle dorsiflexion.

Assessment

Table 1.4   Ankle Dorsiflexion Scores

Score	5	4.5	4	3.5	3.0	2.5	2.0	1.5	1.0	0.5	0
Centimeters	15	13.5	12	10.5	9	7.5	6	4.5	3	1.5	<1.5

Stability Push-Up

Purpose

To assess core stability and pushing strength

Setup

The athlete assumes a prone position on the floor with hands positioned at the level of the collarbones with the fingers pointing forward, knees extended, ankles in neutral, and chin on the floor.

Procedure

- The athlete performs one push-up, rising up as one unit with no sag or elevation in the hips or back (figure 1.5).
- If the athlete does not achieve a score of 4 or 5 (see table 1.5), she performs a push-up from the top down to the lowest range of motion possible and pushes back to the starting position.

Note

The athlete holds the top of the push-up for a couple seconds so the tester can see whether the shoulder blades wing out under load. This part of the test is not scored but can be used to assess scapular stability.

Figure 1.5   Stability push-up.

Assessment

Table 1.5   Scoring Criteria for Stability Push-Up

Score	Criteria
5	Athlete performs push-up with no sag in the hips or sway in the spine.
4	Athlete performs push-up with slightest sag in the hips or sway in the spine.
3	Athlete starts in the top position of the push-up, lowers herself below a 90-degree arm bend, and pushes back up to the starting position with no sag in the hips or sway in the spine.
2	Athlete starts in the top position of the push-up, lowers herself to a 90-degree arm bend, and pushes back up to the starting position with no sag in the hips or sway in the spine.
1	Athlete can't perform a push-up to a 90-degree arm bend or can't keep hips from sagging or spine from swaying.

Ober's Test

Purpose

To assess the length of the tensor fasciae latae and iliotibial band

Setup

The athlete lies on her side on an assessment table. She reaches her upper arm over her head and grasps the bottom of the table, creating tension in the armpit (specifically, the latissimus dorsi muscle). She moves her bottom arm straight out in front of her; then flexes the hip and knee of the bottom leg, forming a 90-degree angle.

Procedure

- The tester stands behind the athlete and uses his hip to stabilize the athlete's pelvis.
- The tester then grasps the ankle of the athlete's upper leg, flexes the knee, and extends the hip.
- With the other hand, the tester feels for the iliotibial band moving over the greater trochanter (figure 1.6a).
- The tester then presses down on the knee to test for spring and tension (figure 1.6b).

Assessment

- Normal tension is indicated if the thigh drops below horizontal or if the knee elicits 15 degrees of spring.

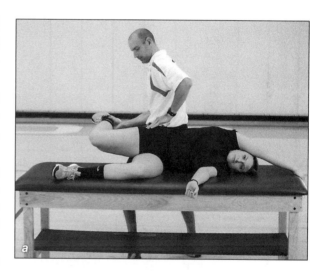

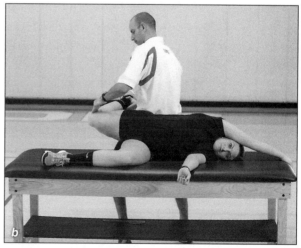

Figure 1.6 Ober's test: (a) tester feels the movement of the iliotibial band over the greater trochanter; (b) tester presses down on the knee.

- Tightness is indicated if the thigh remains abducted or the knee lacks 15 degrees of spring while depressed.
- The iliotibial band also can be palpated with the thumb to identify trigger points.

Note

The iliotibial band is a long band of fascia that runs from the outside of the knee up the side of the thigh and then connects to the pelvis through its insertion into the tensor fasciae latae muscle. The iliotibial band is important because it is a major supporting structure of the knee and can influence the patella's ability to track properly over the joint.

Correction

Iliotibial band release and iliotibial band stretch

Prone Scarecrow

Purpose

To assess active scapular adduction and active external shoulder rotation

Setup

The athlete lies prone on an assessment table with her shoulders abducted and elbows flexed.

Procedure: Retraction

- The athlete's shoulders are flexed at 90 degrees, elbows are off the table and flexed at 90 degrees, and forearms are perpendicular to the table with the hands pointing down.
- The athlete extends at the shoulders and adducts the scapulae.
- The tester places a dowel rod across the elbows and measures the distance from the spine to the bottom of the dowel rod (figure 1.7). See table 1.6 for scoring.

Procedure: Rotation

- The athlete performs the movement for the retraction test and then externally rotates at the shoulders.
- The tester makes sure the athlete keeps the elbows flexed at 90 degrees and the elbows stay in line with the shoulders.
- The tester places a goniometer with the axis at the glenohumeral joint, the fixed arm perpendicular to the floor, and the distal arm parallel to the midline of the lower arm, pointing at the styloid process of the ulna (figure 1.8). See table 1.7 for scoring.

Figure 1.7   Prone scarecrow, retraction.

Figure 1.8   Prone scarecrow, rotation.

Assessment

Table 1.6   Prone Scarecrow, Retraction, Scores

Score	5	4.5	4	3.5	3.0	2.5	2.0	1.5	1.0	0.5	0
Centimeters	10	9	8	7	6	5	4	3	2	1	0

Table 1.7   Prone Scarecrow, Rotation, Scores

Score	5	4	3	2	1	0
Degrees	>90	90-85	84-80	79-75	74-70	<70

Correction

Seated retract and rotate mob

Internal Shoulder Rotation

Purpose

To assess passive internal rotation of the shoulder (with shoulder abducted)

Setup

The athlete lies supine on the table with the low back flat, knees bent, and feet flat on the table. The athlete's shoulder is flexed at 90 degrees, the elbow is off the table and flexed at 90 degrees, and the forearm is perpendicular to the table. The elbow and shoulder must be at the same height. If needed, the tester can place a towel under the distal humerus to level the elbow with the shoulder.

Procedure

- The tester holds the athlete's shoulder down with one hand to prevent substitution of the humeral head in the glenohumeral joint.
- With the other hand, the tester medially rotates the shoulder, bringing the forearm toward the table (figure 1.9).
- The tester places a goniometer with the axis at the glenohumeral joint, the fixed arm perpendicular to the floor, and the distal arm parallel to the midline of the lower arm, pointing at the styloid process of the ulna. See table 1.8 for scoring.

Figure 1.9　Internal shoulder rotation; tester medially rotates the shoulder.

Assessment

A 25-degree decrease of internal shoulder rotation (70 is normal) is classified as glenohumeral internal rotation deficit (GIRD) and has been correlated to a higher likelihood of rotator cuff injuries in overhead throwing and hitting sports.

Table 1.8   Internal Shoulder Rotation Scores

Score	5	4.5	4	3.5	3.0	2.5	2.0	1.5	1.0	0.5	0
Degrees	70	69-65	64-60	59-55	54-50	49-45	44-40	39-35	34-30	29-25	<25

Correction

Posterior shoulder release and sleeper stretch

Scapular Dyskinesis Test (USTA)

Purpose

To assess scapular stability and movement quality

Setup

The athlete stands with her feet under her shoulders, holding 2.5-pound (about 1 kg) weights at her sides, one in each hand, thumbs pointed forward.

Procedure

- Keeping the elbows extended and the thumbs pointed up, the athlete elevates both of her arms in the scapular plane to their end range of motion (figure 1.10).
- The athlete holds the end range of motion for 2 seconds and then slowly lowers her arms back to her sides in the scapular plane. The tester observes the movement of the shoulder blades and notes any winging or overuse of the neck and upper trapezius muscles during both ascent and descent. The tester notes any asymmetry; this is especially important during the descent phase.

Figure 1.10   Scapular dyskinesis test.

Scapular Dyskinesis System Used to Categorize Abnormal Scapular Motion Pattern Definitions

Inferior angle (type I): At rest, the inferior medial scapular border may be prominent dorsally. During arm motion, the inferior angle tilts dorsally and the acromion tilts ventrally over the top of the thorax. The axis of the rotation is in the horizontal plane.

Medial border (type II): At rest, the entire medial border may be prominent dorsally. During arm motion, the medial scapular border tilts dorsally off the thorax. The axis of the rotation is vertical in the frontal plane.

Superior border (type III): At rest, the superior border of the scapula may be elevated and the scapula can also be anteriorly displaced. During arm motion, a shoulder shrug initiates movement without significant winging of the scapular occurring. The axis of this motion occurs in the sagittal plane.

Symmetric scapulohumeral (type IV): At rest, the position of both scapulae are relatively symmetrical, taking into account that the dominant arm may be slightly lower. During arm motion, the scapulae rotate symmetrically upward such that the inferior angles translate laterally away from the midline and the scapular medial border remains flush against the thoracic wall. The reverse occurs during lowering of the arm.

Reprinted from *Journal of Shoulder and Elbow Surgery*, 11(6), W.B. Kibler, T.L. Uhl, J.W.Q. Maddux, et al., "Qualitative clinical evaluation of scapular dysfunction: A reliability study," 550-556, 2002, with permission from Elsevier.

Correction

Scapular adduction exercises

LANDING COMPETENCY

The landing competency assessment is broken down into three parts: continuous squat jump, knee tuck jump, and single-leg hurdle hop. All three tests evaluate the athlete's ability to maintain proper joint alignment while decelerating or transferring force into the floor. The inability to maintain proper joint alignment in these basic movements in a controlled setting puts the athlete at a higher risk for lower-extremity injuries. The landing competency tests should be recorded from the front view to better evaluate joint alignment in slow motion.

Continuous Squat Jump

Purpose

To assess dynamic joint stability in a dynamic squat movement and during bilateral jumping

Setup

Tape a line on the floor. The athlete stands with feet shoulder-width apart, toes pointing forward, and feet on the line.

Procedure

- The athlete squats down to her end range of motion (figure 1.11*a*) and then performs a jump to maximal height (figure 1.11*b*).
- When the feet touch the floor, the athlete sinks back into a squat and repeats.
- The athlete attempts five jumps. See table 1.9 for scoring.

Figure 1.11 Continuous squat jump: *(a)* athlete squats down; *(b)* athlete jumps to maximal height.

Assessment

Table 1.9　Scoring Criteria for Continuous Squat Jump

Score	Criteria
5	Athlete maintains good torso posture; even weight distribution between legs; and alignment of foot, knee, and hip.
4	Slight deviation of torso posture or foot, knee, or hip alignment.
3	Moderate deviation in torso posture or foot, knee, or hip alignment.
2	Gross deviation in torso posture; weight distribution between legs; and alignment of foot, knee, or hip.
1	Continual knocking of the knees during squat jumps.

Knee Tuck Jump

Purpose

To assess dynamic joint stability in a bilateral stance with increased force displacement into the floor

Setup

Tape a line on the floor. The athlete stands with feet directly under hips, toes pointing forward, and feet on the line (figure 1.12a).

Procedure

- The athlete jumps in the air and raises his knees to his chest (figure 1.12b).
- The athlete performs eight repetitions continuously.
- The athlete focuses on limiting floor contact time between jumps and getting maximal height on each jump.
- The tester makes sure the athlete is raising his knees to his chest, not his heels to his butt. See table 1.10 for scoring.

Figure 1.12   Knee tuck jump: *(a)* starting position; *(b)* tuck jump.

Assessment

Table 1.10   Scoring Criteria for Knee Tuck Jump

Score	Criteria
5	Foot, knee, and ankle stay aligned. Athlete jumps and lands in roughly the same spot throughout the test.
4	Slight deviation in alignment.
3	Moderate deviation in alignment.
2	Gross deviation in alignment.
1	Knocked knees throughout the eight repetitions.

Single-Leg Hurdle Hop

Purpose

To assess single-leg dynamic stability and deceleration

Setup

Tape two lines on the floor 28 inches (70 cm) apart. Center a 6- or 12-inch (15 or 30 cm) hurdle between the two lines. The athlete stands behind one line on one leg.

Procedure

- The athlete jumps off one leg over the hurdle (figure 1.13a) landing on the same leg and clearing the second line with his heel (figure 1.13b).
- The athlete sticks the landing on one leg for 2 to 3 seconds.
- The athlete completes three attempts on each leg.
- The tester scores each jump separately (see table 1.11) and then averages the scores to come up with an overall score for each leg.

Figure 1.13 Single-leg hurdle hop: (a) hop over the hurdle; (b) land past the second line.

Assessment

Table 1.11 Scoring Criteria for Single-Leg Hurdle Hop

Score	Criteria
5	Foot, knee, and ankle aligned. Pelvis remains flat and shoulders stay over hips.
4	Slight deviation of the criteria for a score of 5.
3	Moderate deviation of the criteria for a score of 5.
2	Gross deviation of the criteria for a score of 5, or athlete hops or instep of foot comes off the floor.
1	Athlete is unable to balance at all on landing.

JOINT-BY-JOINT BREAKDOWN

If a score of 4 or 5 is not achieved in the movement screen for the overhead squat, single-leg squat, ankle dorsiflexion, or prone scarecrow, additional testing is required. Table 1.12 indicates additional tests that need to be performed when a satisfactory score isn't achieved in these movement tests.

Table 1.12 Additional Tests for Unsatisfactory Scores

	Overhead squat	Single-leg squat	Ankle dorsiflexion	Prone scarecrow
Shoulder flexion and T-spine integration test	X			
Active shoulder flexion	X			
Trunk extension	X			
Half-kneeling ankle dorsiflexion	X			
Supine hip flexion	X			
Supine external hip rotation	X	X		
Supine internal hip rotation	X	X		
Pectoralis major				X
Pectoralis minor				X
Gastrocnemius			X	
Soleus			X	
Thomas test	X	X		

The joint-by-joint breakdown tests are compared against goniometric norms or are subjectively assessed using (+) or (–) to denote a positive or negative test.

Shoulder Flexion and T-Spine Integration Test

Purpose

To assess the ability to reverse the curve of the midthoracic spine during maximal shoulder flexion

Setup

The athlete stands with her arms at her sides, elbows locked, and thumbs pointed forward.

Procedure

- Keeping the elbows locked, the athlete slowly moves the arms into maximal shoulder flexion (figure 1.14).
- The tester stands behind the athlete to assess movement at the midthoracic spine with shoulder flexion.

Assessment

A positive test is recorded if the athlete doesn't reverse the curve of the thoracic spine.

Correction

Thoracic mob (peanut)

Figure 1.14 Shoulder flexion and T-spine integration test.

Active Shoulder Flexion

Purpose

To assess active shoulder flexion

Setup

The athlete stands upright, feet hip-width apart, elbows extended, arms at her sides, and thumbs pointed forward.

Procedure

- Keeping the elbows locked, the athlete flexes the upper arms at the shoulders (figure 1.15).

- The tester has the athlete stop arm flexion at end range of motion or if the low back increases its curve or the chest elevates toward the ceiling.

Assessment

Normal active shoulder flexion is 180 degrees of arm flexion without elevation of the chest or rib cage.

Correction

Lat release, shoulder flexion mob, and PNF shoulder flexion

Figure 1.15   Active shoulder flexion.

Trunk Extension

Purpose

To assess the ability to extend through the thoracic spine

Setup

The athlete stands with her arms at her sides, elbows bent at 90 degrees, and knees in neutral.

Procedure

Keeping the elbows bent, the athlete flexes at the shoulders and performs a back bend while trying to elevate her chest and rib cage toward the ceiling (figure 1.16).

Assessment

The athlete should easily be able to get the ASIS (front hip bones) past

Figure 1.16   Trunk extension: back bend.

the toes and the shoulders past the heels. The back should form a slight C shape.

Correction

Thoracic mob (foam roll)

Half-Kneeling Ankle Dorsiflexion

Purpose

To assess closed-chain ankle dorsiflexion with the knee flexed at 90 degrees

Setup

Facing a wall, the athlete kneels on a pad on one knee and on the other side flexes the hip and knee and places the foot flat on the floor. This creates a 90-degree angle with both legs. The tester places a ruler in front of the athlete's longest toe.

Procedure

- Keeping the front foot flat and heel down, the athlete dorsiflexes the foot, pushing the knee forward toward the wall while keeping the kneecap centered over the middle toe (figure 1.17).
- The athlete moves closer to or farther away from the wall until the knee just contacts the wall and the foot remains flat on the floor.
- The tester measures the distance from the athlete's longest toe to the wall.

Assessment

Normal kneeling ankle dorsiflexion would allow the knee to travel 4 inches (10 cm) past the toe.

Figure 1.17   Half-kneeling ankle dorsiflexion.

Correction

Half-kneeling ankle mob

Supine Hip Flexion

Purpose

To assess passive hip flexion

Setup

The athlete lies supine on an assessment table. The tester places one hand, palm up, between the assessment table and the athlete's lumbar spine.

Procedure

- The tester flexes one of the athlete's knees and then flexes the same hip to the athlete's end range of motion or when the lumbar spine flattens to the assessment table.
- The tester places a goniometer with the axis point at the femoral greater trochanter, the fixed arm parallel to the midline of the trunk, and the distal arm parallel to the midline of the thigh (figure 1.18).

Assessment

Normal hip flexion is 135 degrees. The tester also should feel for tension. Does the joint restriction come abruptly and then just stop, or is it a more gradual increase in tension?

Correction

PNF supine hip flexion stretch (band) and forearm to instep complex

Figure 1.18   Supine hip flexion.

Supine External Hip Rotation

Purpose

To assess passive external hip rotation

Setup

The athlete lies supine on an assessment table.

Procedure

- The tester flexes the athlete's knee and hip to 90 degrees.
- The tester then places one hand on the outside of the knee and one hand on the outside of the lateral malleolus (ankle bone) (figure 1.19).
- Stabilizing the knee with one hand, the tester applies pressure at the ankle toward the midline.
- The tester places the goniometer with the axis point at the midpatella, the fixed arm parallel to the axis of the femur, and the distal arm parallel to the long axis of the tibia.

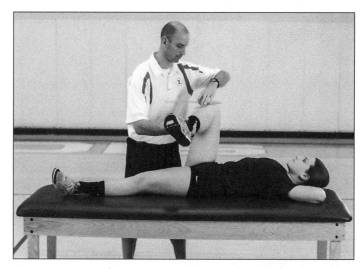

Figure 1.19 Supine external hip rotation.

Assessment

Normal range of motion is 45 to 60 degrees.

Correction

Piriformis release and PNF standing piriformis stretch

Supine Internal Hip Rotation

Purpose

To assess passive internal hip rotation

Setup

The athlete lies supine on an assessment table.

Procedure

- The tester flexes the athlete's knee and hip to 90 degrees.
- The tester then places one hand on the inside of the knee and grasps the ankle with the other hand.
- Stabilizing the inside of the knee, the tester applies pressure at the ankle, rotating the lower leg out, away from the midline of the body (figure 1.20).
- The tester places the goniometer with the axis point at the midpatella, the fixed arm parallel to the long axis of the femur, and the distal arm parallel to the long axis of the tibia.

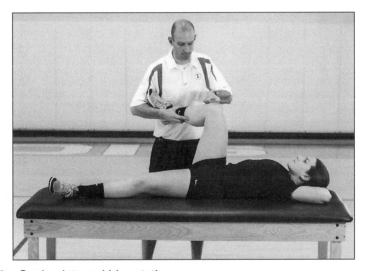

Figure 1.20   Supine internal hip rotation.

Assessment

Normal range of motion is 40 to 45 degrees.

Correction

Three-position groin rock

Pectoralis Major

Purpose

To assess the length tension of the pectoralis major muscle

Setup

The athlete lies supine on an assessment table.

Procedure

The athlete interlocks the fingers and places the hands behind the head.

Assessment

Normal range of motion is indicated if the athlete's elbows lie relaxed on the table (figure 1.21). Tightness is indicated if the elbows are elevated off the table.

Correction

Pectoralis release and pectoralis major stretch

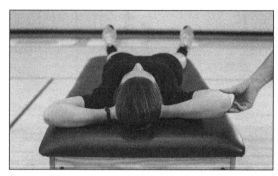

Figure 1.21 Pectoralis major: the athlete's left elbow shows normal range of motion, and the athlete would exhibit tightness if shoulder were raised, as shown on the right.

Pectoralis Minor

Purpose

To assess the length tension of the pectoralis minor muscle

Setup

The athlete lies supine on an assessment table with arms down at the sides and knuckles facing up.

Procedure

- The tester stands at the head of the table and compares the athlete's shoulder heights.
- A measurement from the spine of the scapula just under the acromion to the table is taken in centimeters (figure 1.22).

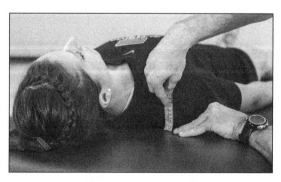

Figure 1.22 Pectoralis minor.

- Finally, the tester applies downward pressure on each shoulder to see if there are any differences in tension from right to left.

Assessment

The tester notes positive differences in shoulder height or tension. The normal measure from the spine of the scapula to the table is 2 centimeters.

Note

An athlete with a lot of muscle bulk in the rear deltoid or back might have a distance greater than 2 centimeters and receive a false positive in this test.

Correction

Pectoralis release and pectoralis minor stretch

Gastrocnemius (Two Joints)

Purpose

To assess the length tension of the gastrocnemius muscle

Setup

The athlete lies prone on an assessment table with the feet and ankles off the end of the table.

Procedure

- With the athlete's knees extended, the tester dorsiflexes the athlete's foot to talus neutral (figure 1.23).
- Range of motion is from talus neutral to maximal dorsiflexion.
- The tester places the goniometer with the axis point at the lateral calcaneus under the lateral

Figure 1.23   Gastrocnemius.

malleolus, the fixed arm parallel to the long axis of the fibula, and the distal arm parallel to the lateral border of the foot.

Assessment

Normal range is 10 to 15 degrees.

Correction

Plantar fascia release, calf release, and straight-leg calf stretch

Soleus (One Joint)

Purpose

To assess the length tension of the soleus muscle

Setup

The athlete lies prone on an assessment table with the feet and ankles off the end of the table. The knee is flexed to 90 degrees, giving slack to both the gastrocnemius and plantaris.

Procedure

Figure 1.24   Soleus.

- The tester holds the athlete's ankle with one hand and moves the foot to talus neutral with the other hand (figure 1.24).
- Range of motion is measured from talus neutral to maximal dorsiflexion.
- The tester places the goniometer with the axis point at the lateral calcaneus under the lateral malleolus, the fixed arm parallel to the long axis of the fibula, and the distal arm parallel to the lateral border of the foot.

Assessment

Normal range is 20 degrees.

Correction

Plantar fascia release, calf release, and bent-leg calf stretch

Thomas Test

Purpose

To assess the length tension of one- and two-joint hip flexors

Setup

The athlete leans against the very end of an assessment table so that her feet are on the floor and her butt is barely on the end of the table. The athlete then pulls one knee into her chest. She then lies back on the table with her knee pulled into her chest.

Procedure

- The tester adjusts the flexed leg so that the low back and sacrum just flatten out on the table.
- The athlete is now asked to relax the hip and knee of the leg hanging off the table (figure 1.25).

Assessment

The leg hanging off the table is the one being assessed.

Figure 1.25 Thomas test: *(a)* psoas; *(b)* rectus femoris.

One-joint hip flexors (psoas, iliacus): The tester places the goniometer with the axis point at the greater trochanter, the fixed arm parallel to the table, and the distal arm parallel to the midline of the thigh, arm pointing at the center of the knee joint. Tightness is indicated if the hip is flexed, causing the thigh to be elevated higher than the table. Normal length is indicated with the hip from 0 to 5 degrees of extension. This is shown with the thigh parallel or just below parallel to the floor or straight out from or on a slight descent from the table. Excessive length is indicated if the hip drops below the table more than 10 degrees.

Two-joint hip flexors (rectus femoris): The tester places the goniometer with the axis point at the axis of the knee, the fixed arm parallel to the midline of the thigh, and the distal arm parallel to the midline of the lower leg, pointing at the lateral malleolus. Normal length is indicated when the thigh and lower leg create a 90- to 95-degree angle.

Correction

One joint: half-kneeling psoas stretch (band)

Two joints: rectus femoris release, rectus femoris stretch

SUMMARY

The goal of the individual assessment is to uncover marked deficits in mobility or stability that create inefficient movement or put the athlete at a higher risk for injury. The results of the movement screen and the joint-by-joint breakdown are used to prescribe corrective exercises for each athlete. The number of exercises and volume performed in each session and during each week depends on the number of positive findings and the severity of the deficits. In most cases, the corrective exercises are performed before, during, or after training and practice. Corrective exercises consist of myofascial releases, mobilizations, stretches, and muscle activation exercises. When the corrective exercises are implemented depends on what is restricted and what exercises or movements are being performed in the training session. If a restricted joint or movement hampers performance in an exercise, drill, or practice or puts the athlete at a higher risk of injury, corrective exercises should be performed prior to training or at least prior to the exercise that it affects. If the restriction doesn't affect the current training session, corrective exercises can be performed after the session. For example, an athlete with a restriction in shoulder flexion should mobilize the shoulder prior to performing overhead exercises such as the snatch and the overhead press. In another example, an ankle that is restricted in dorsiflexion should be mobilized prior to performing any kind of squat motion. Corrective exercises are presented and described in chapter 3, Mobility.

Chapter 2

Performance Testing and Data Collection

Performance testing and data collection are important components of the training process for both the coaching staff and the athlete. They provide the coaching staff with empirical data on each athletes' progress so they can determine load prescriptions and individual goals to ensure the success of the overall program. For the athlete, they provide tangible evidence that hard work is paying off, provide motivation to reach new personal bests, and foster positive competitiveness with teammates.

Most testing protocols are based on pre- and posttesting—that is, testing during the first and last weeks of a training period. The major drawback of this method is that the test results give a snapshot of performance only at the beginning and the end of the training period and do not evaluate the work done in between. As a result, the athlete's performance and improvement, and the success of the whole program, are based on numbers collected on two occasions, not during the entire 14- to 18-week training period.

Many variables affect an athlete's level of performance in a given session, such as nutrition, sleep, stress, and recovery from previous workouts, practices, and matches. Testing frequently gives the coach more data points over a period of time, resulting in a more valid assessment of overall progress. Off-season testing consists of four biweekly court performance tests, six core lifts in the weight room that are tracked each session they are performed, and body composition testing, which generally occurs twice a semester but can be administered more for athletes for whom changing body composition is a major priority. With the exception of body composition testing, this provides 8 to 16 data points to use to evaluate athletes' progress and the program's overall success.

In-season, tracking core lifts remains a priority, but court performance testing is limited to biweekly vertical jump testing because of time constraints and the need to manage overall training volume. Performance testing in-season may be uncommon, but it can be a valuable asset to a program. It helps the coach determine whether athletes are maintaining their levels of power output and acceleration. A significant drop in these variables can mean that the training program is not effective or that the athletes are not recovering properly as a result of training or competition volume.

COURT PERFORMANCE

Court performance is tested weekly or biweekly in the off-season prior to plyometric or agility training. Variables tested are vertical explosiveness, horizontal explosiveness, and acceleration. The tests used to assess these variables are the no-step vertical jump, approach jump, broad jump, and pro agility tests.

Vertical jump is measured using two tests: the no-step vertical jump test and the approach jump test. Before either test is administered, the athlete's standing reach is measured.

Standing Reach

Purpose

An athlete's standing reach is needed to calculate how high the athlete actually gets off the floor during the vertical jump test. This is done by subtracting the athlete's standing reach from height touched during testing.

Setup

Attach a tape measure to a wall or tape with increments written on it.

Procedure

- The athlete aligns the lateral border of one foot and hip against the wall.
- With the hand closest the wall, the athlete reaches as high as possible up the wall.
- The athlete touches the high point with the palm of the hand and the fingers flat against the wall.
- The tester records the height reached.

No-Step Vertical Jump

Purpose

To measure vertical power output

Setup

Prepare a Vertec device (recommended) or a similar jump testing device.

Procedure

- The athlete stands with the feet shoulder-width apart, the toes parallel to the base of the Vertec, the shoulders and hips directly under the vanes, and the hands above the head.
- The athlete starts the movement by descending into a squat and bringing the arms down and back, extending at the shoulder (figure 2.1*a*).
- At the bottom of the squat, the athlete reverses direction and explodes up, touching the highest vane with the dominant hand (figure 2.1*b*).

Figure 2.1   No-step vertical jump: *(a)* athlete descends into a squat; *(b)* athlete explodes up and touches the vanes with the dominant hand.

- During the setup and the descent into the squat, there must be no foot movement. If a foot moves or the athlete takes a step, the jump is not valid and should not be recorded.
- The athlete receives three attempts.
- Vertical jump is calculated by subtracting the standing reach height from the best vertical jump measure. See table 2.1.

Assessment

Table 2.1   No-Step Vertical Jump, Division I College Volleyball

Category	Male (inches)	Female (inches)
Excellent	30 and above	22 and above
Average	25 to 29	18 to 21
Below average	Less than 25	Less than 18

Approach Jump

Purpose

To measure how high an athlete can touch. The approach jump is more sport specific than the no-step vertical jump test because it allows the athlete to use an approach, as she would in on-court situations. This is not a measure of power output, but rather, of how high the athlete can touch while attacking.

Setup

Prepare a Vertec device or a similar jump testing device.

Procedure

- The athlete starts a maximum of 15 feet (4.6 m) from the Vertec and performs an attack approach (figure 2.2*a*) to jump and touch the highest vane possible with the dominant hand (figure 2.2*b*).
- The athlete receives three attempts, and the best result is recorded. See table 2.2.

Assessment

Table 2.2   Approach Jump, Division I College Volleyball

Category	Male (inches)	Female (inches)
Excellent	35 and above	25 and above
Average	28 to 34.9	20.5 to 24.9
Below average	Less than 28	Less than 20.5

Figure 2.2 Approach jump: *(a)* athlete performs an attack approach; *(b)* athlete jumps and touches the highest vanes possible.

Broad Jump

Purpose

To measure horizontal power output

Equipment

Measuring tape, yardstick, court tape.

Setup

The starting line can be a line already on the court, or you can tape one down. Extend a tape measure from the front of the starting line out to 12 feet (3.7 m). Tape the tape measure to the floor so it doesn't move.

Procedure

- The athlete stands with feet shoulder-width apart, toes pointed forward behind the starting line, and hands above the head.
- The athlete swings his arms down and back as he performs a quarter to half squat (figure 2.3a).
- He then rapidly swings his arms forward and jumps off both feet as far forward as possible (figure 2.3b).
- The athlete lands on both feet and a measurement is taken from the starting line to the closest heel. This is done by placing the yardstick against the heel closer to the starting line and perpendicular to the measuring tape. See table 2.3.
- If the athlete falls backward, puts a hand down, or does not stick the landing, the jump is not counted, and the athlete does another repetition.
- The athlete performs three jumps.

Figure 2.3   Broad jump: (a) athlete swings the arms back and down and squats; (b) athlete jumps forward as far as possible.

Assessment

Table 2.3   Broad Jump, Division I College Volleyball

Category	Male (inches)	Female (inches)
Excellent	110 and above	90 and above
Average	94 to 109	75 to 89
Below average	Less than 94	Less than 75

Pro Agility Using the Width of the Volleyball Court

Purpose

To measure the ability to accelerate and decelerate

Equipment

Video camera and Dartfish or a similar software, or a stopwatch

Setup

Tape a 3-foot (1 m) line perpendicular to the center line, dividing the volleyball court in half. This is done by measuring 14 feet, 9 inches (4.5 m) in from the sideline. If you are measuring time with a video camera, set up the tripod so the camera is pointing directly down the taped-down line dividing the center of the court.

Starting Position

The athlete straddles the 3-foot (1 m) line in an athletic stance.

Procedure

- The athlete sprints to the left sideline.
- She touches the sideline with her left foot and then turns and sprints crosscourt to the opposite sideline.
- She touches the line with her left foot and sprints back through the starting line.
- The test is repeated with the athlete first sprinting to the right.
- The best time of two trials right and two trials left are recorded. See table 2.4.

Note

The tester can time the athlete using a standard stopwatch or, to increase accuracy, video the test and use Dartfish or a similar software to get a more definitive time.

Assessment

Scores starting left and right can be compared to identify imbalances in acceleration between legs.

Table 2.4   Pro Agility, Division I College Volleyball

Category	Male (seconds)	Female (seconds)
Excellent	4.35 or less	4.84 or less
Average	4.36 to 4.50	4.85 to 5.22
Below average	4.51 or more	5.23 or more

THE VOLLEYBALL PERFORMANCE INDEX

The American Volleyball Coaches Association (AVCA) uses the Volleyball Performance Index (VPI), a compilation of eight measurable physical indicators that are positively correlated with success as a volleyball player: height, reach, standing vertical jump, block touch, height of attack, arm swing speed (velocity), acceleration, and lateral agility (pro agility). A player's plot point on each test is based on variance from the mean of the sample. Each test is weighted equally, and the rescaled values are added and multiplied by 100 to produce a player's VPI, or aptitude score. The following table shows a sample of the testing metrics that aggregate into a 664 AVCA VPI score.

Height	Reach	Standing vertical jump	Block touch	Attack height	Velocity	Acceleration (15 ft, or 4.5 m)	Pro agility (15, 30, 15 ft, or 4.5, 9, 4.5 m)
6ft, 5 in. (196 cm)	8ft, 5.5 in. (258 cm)	21.5 in. (54. 6 cm)	9ft, 11.5 in. (304 cm)	10 ft, 1 in. (307 cm)	44.18 mph (19.7 km/h)	1.07 sec	5.17 sec

Most starters in elite Division I programs have a VPI of 550 or higher. Arm swing velocity is a key differentiator among middles and outsides, with 32 miles per hour (51.5 km/h) as a separating metric. Attack height is also key (9 ft, 5 in., or 287 cm, is a significant benchmark). The exceptions to the 550 standard usually are setters and liberos. For setters, vertical jump, arm swing speed, acceleration, and pro agility—the four factors in the VPI that reflect general athleticism—were more significant than the height metrics. The higher-rated liberos had higher standing vertical jumps, faster arms, and better pro agility scores—again, three measures of overall athleticism—than those rated lower. For more information, go to www.avca.org.

WEIGHT ROOM

Performance goals in the weight room are focused on the development of lower-body strength and power. Projected back squat, front squat, and box step-up maximums are used to evaluate lower-body strength. Projected hang snatch, power snatch, jump shrug, and push jerk maximums are used to evaluate power output. In the weight room, there is never a designated test day. Rather, every day is a test day. Instead of dedicating a whole session to testing, the numbers achieved in the athlete's last set are recorded and a projected maximum is calculated. To validate the results, the strength coach must watch the last set of each exercise to evaluate technique, range of motion, and speed of movement (snatch and jump shrug), and to confirm the weight being lifted. If technique or range of motion are lacking in the set, the athlete is not credited with the weight corresponding to the 1-repetition maximum (1RM). See the 1RM chart in the back of the book for more complete data.

Some of the benefits of data collection over pretesting or posttesting are that a training session is not wasted on testing alone, athletes don't have to attempt heavy lifts when they don't have the proper base of training to do so properly, and performance can be systematically assessed during each session. Moreover, it enables coaches and athletes to choose appropriate loads for the next session.

The use of data collection to manipulate strength-based exercise 1RMs and prescribe loads for the next workout is handled by using estimates, exercise to failure, or an autoregulatory training method. All three methods manipulate the 1RM based on performance, but they are implemented in different ways.

In the estimate method, the athlete performs the last set of an exercise at a given weight and repetition range. Upon completion of the repetition range, the athlete estimates how many more repetitions she could have achieved with proper technique. In the exercise to failure method, the athlete performs her last set with the prescribed weight just before or to failure. The autoregulatory method can be performed when the last two sets of an exercise use the same repetition range and intensity. Either the athlete performs the prescribed number of repetitions and estimates how many more she could achieve, or she performs the prescribed weights to failure. Then the weight of the final set is manipulated based on the estimated number of reps they could have achieved or the number of repetitions performed over the prescribed repetition range. This allows for an in-session manipulation of the athlete's 1RM to provide the most accurate load prescription. Table 2.5 shows how to manipulate a 1RM based on how many repetitions are estimated or achieved beyond a prescribed repetition range.

Usually, the estimate method is used when controlling training volume and fatigue is a priority, such as during the preseason, in-season, or off-season competition and at the beginning of off-season training cycles. The exercise to failure method is used mostly in the heart of off-season training. The autoregulatory method is used in the off-season when the number of repetitions is 5 and fewer.

The adjustment of 1RM and load prescription for power-based exercises is handled differently than strength-based data collection. Bar speed and technique are the major indicators of whether the athlete is ready to

Table 2.5 Manipulation of 1RM Based on Repetitions Estimated or Achieved

Repetitions past range	Change in 1RM or weight on last set
−4 or 5	−10 lb
−2 or 3	−5 lb
0	0
+2 or 3	+5 lb
+4 to 6	+10 lb
+7 to 10	+15 lb

increase her projected maximum and move up in weight in the following workout. An adjustment of 5 to 10 pounds (2.3 to 4.5 kg) can have a major impact in an exercise such as the snatch as a result of the distance the bar must travel at a high velocity. More objective data can be obtained on bar speed with the use of Tendo units. The most important thing to remember is not to sacrifice bar speed for weight.

SELF DATA COLLECTION

On all weight training accessory exercises, the athlete should record in a workout book the weight and repetitions performed for each exercise in her weight training program. She can then look back in her workout book to remember what weight she used in the previous session and track her progress in all of the exercises. She can also note in her book whether she should stay at a certain weight or increase weight in the next session. If an athlete has difficulty performing a body weight exercise such as a push-up or chin-up, she can use a band to decrease the percentage of her body weight that she must lift. She can then decrease the amount of resistance until she can perform the exercise lifting her full body weight. She should write down not only how many repetitions she performed but also the color band she used (the colors correspond to resistance levels). The goal is to get better every day. If an athlete can perform an exercise with proper technique, she should increase the load, repetitions, and difficulty to promote physical adaptation. Self data collection on every exercise helps athletes know where they are and the next step in their progress.

BODY COMPOSITION

The evaluation of body composition is not a performance test, but it is important because body weight can have a huge impact on performance. Body composition is usually expressed in body fat percentage. This number indicates the percentage of the person's body weight that is fat. Athletes should maintain or work to achieve a body fat percentage that is both healthy and conducive to optimal performance. The ideal body fat range for male athletes is 8 to 15 percent; for female athletes it is 15 to 22 percent. A body fat percentage over 18 percent for males and 25 percent for females is a concern because of the extra load on joints when landing and the potential loss of vertical power output due to excessive, unproductive weight.

The best way to adjust body composition is to assess the person's current diet and prescribe a nutrition plan based on her particular needs. An exercise program to reduce body fat can be implemented, but it should be interval and rest based, not aerobic. Volleyball is a power sport that benefits from fast-twitch, explosive muscle fibers. If training involves lower-intensity, long-duration exercise, muscle fibers may adapt to be more endurance based rather than explosive. Therefore, aerobic exercises would not be ideal for volleyball athletes trying to reduce body fat percentage.

Body composition can be tested in many ways. Underwater weighing is the gold standard because it is the most accurate. However, it is usually available only in performance labs and is difficult to administer or perform. The Bod Pod provides almost identical measures as underwater weighing and is easy to administer. However, pods are expensive and not accessible to everyone. Skinfold calipers are fairly accurate when used by trained individuals but have poor inter-tester reliability. Skinfold tests are easy to administer, though, and calipers are fairly inexpensive.

These modalities may or may not be available at universities, schools, and training facilities. Coaches and athletes should choose the modality that is most accessible.

SUMMARY

Performance testing and weight room data collection provide the strength coach and coaching staff with objective feedback on the effectiveness of the training program and accurate individualized load prescriptions for core weight room exercises. Body composition is an important component of performance and joint health and should be assessed in the most accurate and accessible modality available.

Part II

TRAINING

In chapters 3 through 9 you will learn about the importance of a variety of performance modalities as well as exercises for improving them.

Volleyball is a power sport. Therefore, performance training needs to focus primarily on improving vertical jump ability as well as the ability to react and accelerate quickly and efficiently in multiple planes of movement. To enhance and optimize these abilities, training must address multiplane balance and stability, strength, power, the core, agility, and conditioning. All of these components are significant pieces to the puzzle and build on each other to maximize the training effect. The components are not necessarily equal in terms of volume and emphasis, but if a single variable is left out or overlooked, the result suffers. In chapters 4 through 9, you will learn about the importance of a variety of performance modalities as well as exercises for improving them.

Chapter 3

Mobility

Mobility is the foundation to building efficient, strong, explosive, and injury-resistant volleyball players. The body is linked head to toe through bones, joints, connective tissue, and muscles. These structures produce movement by working together synergistically to create and transfer energy. If there is a block in even one link, the whole system suffers. A single immobile joint or tight muscle can affect all the joints above or below it and the motion they create together. For example, a marked restriction in ankle dorsiflexion affects the athlete's ability to squat and create efficient angles to accelerate and decelerate, and decreases the athlete's overall power output because of improper preloading. For athletes to achieve optimal performance on the court, immobilities must be reduced or negated and normal movement maintained through the implementation of myofascial releases, joint mobilizations, stretching, or a combination of these.

MYOFASCIAL RELEASE

Fascia is a fibrous connective tissue that surrounds muscles, joints, and bones. It functions to reduce friction so muscles can slide and glide between each other and over structures as well as to transmit mechanical tension produced by muscle or outside forces. Healthy fascia has an elastic property that allows freedom of movement.

Fascia can be compromised as a result of trauma, poor posture, poor movement mechanics, lack of recovery, or nutritional factors causing areas in the tissue to become dense and inelastic. The result is a lack of range of motion, inefficient movement, and, in some cases, pain or injury. The inelastic, thickened fascia is referred to as a trigger point. Usually, trigger points are painful when compressed and can send referred pain to other parts of the body.

Modalities for improving myofascial pliability and reducing trigger points are called myofascial release techniques. These techniques require the use of compression or pressure to lengthen and create pliability in the tissue and increase blood circulation in the areas being treated. This chapter describes self myofascial release techniques that can be performed without assistance, can be implemented in large groups, and use relatively inexpensive equipment such as foam rollers, golf balls, softballs, lacrosse balls, and trigger point sticks. Self myofascial release techniques can cause a considerable amount of discomfort. This is common and decreases with consistent implementation of a proper program and improved soft tissue health.

Plantar Fascia Release

Equipment

Golf ball

Starting Position

Stand with a golf ball under the arch of one foot.

Procedure

- Shift body weight onto the foot with the ball under it.
- Roll the ball forward and backward under the arch of the foot.
- If a specific area on the bottom of the foot is painful, apply direct pressure on the area with the ball until the discomfort decreases or subsides.

Calf and Achilles Tendon (Stick)

Equipment

Trigger point stick

Starting Position

Sit on a bench or chair.

Procedure

- Using a trigger point stick, apply pressure to the back of the lower leg.

- Maintain pressure and roll the stick up and down, targeting the Achilles tendon as well as the medial and lateral heads of the gastrocnemius.
- Focus attention on areas that feel knotted or uncomfortable.

Note

Sit so the muscles of the lower leg are relaxed during the release.

Calf and Achilles Tendon (Barbell)

Equipment

Barbell with no plates on it

Starting Position

Place a barbell on the floor. Sit on the floor with the legs straight and one lower leg on top of the barbell.

Procedure

- Cross one leg over the other to create more pressure on the target leg (figure 3.1).
- Place the hands on the floor for support and lift the butt off the floor.
- Roll forward and backward over the bar from the ankle to the calf.
- If a trigger point or area of increased discomfort is found, apply constant pressure over the area with the bar until the pain or soreness subsides or decreases.

Figure 3.1   Calf and Achilles tendon (barbell): crossing one leg over the other to create more pressure.

Rectus Femoris Release

Equipment

Softball

Starting Position

Lie prone with the forearms on the floor and parallel to the torso. Place a ball under the thigh just above the kneecap. Cross the foot of the uninvolved leg over the ankle of the involved leg to increase the pressure of the ball into the thigh.

Procedure

- Slowly roll up and down the center of the upper leg from the starting position to the hip bone.
- If a trigger point or area of increased discomfort is found, apply constant pressure over the area with the ball until the pain or soreness subsides or decreases.

Lateral Quad Release

Equipment

6-inch (15 cm) foam roll

Starting Position

Lie on one side supported by the forearm. Place a foam roll perpendicular to the body under the upper leg just above the knee. Rotate the body slightly forward so pressure is on the lateral quadriceps (figure 3.2).

Figure 3.2   Lateral quad release; foam roll under upper leg with pressure on the lateral quadriceps.

Procedure

- Option 1: Roll slowly from the knee to the hip.
- Option 2: At a moderate pace with a slight up-and-down movement, roll from the knee to the hip.
- With either option, take 30 seconds to 2 minutes to move from the knee to the hip.
- If a trigger point or area of increased discomfort is found, stop rolling and target the area with constant pressure until the pain or soreness subsides or decreases.

IT Band

Equipment

6-inch (15 cm) foam roll

Starting Position

Lie on one side supported by the forearm. Place a foam roll perpendicular to the body under the upper leg just above the knee (figure 3.3).

Figure 3.3   IT band; foam roll under upper leg.

Procedure

- Option 1: Roll slowly from the knee to the hip.
- Option 2: At a moderate pace with a slight up-and-down movement, roll from the knee to the hip.
- With either option, take 30 seconds to 2 minutes to move from the knee to the hip.
- If a trigger point or area of increased discomfort is found, stop rolling and target the area with constant pressure until the pain or soreness subsides or decreases.

Hamstring Muscle Origin

Equipment

Lacrosse ball and a box, bench, or hard chair

Starting Position

Sit on a box, bench, or hard chair with a lacrosse ball just anterior to the bones you sit on (ischial tuberosity).

Procedure

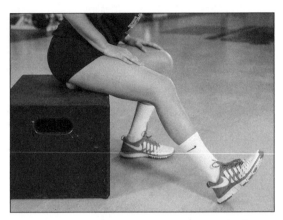

Figure 3.4   Hamstring muscle origin; ball under hips.

- Lean forward at the hip to roll on top of the ball, lifting the butt off the box, bench, or chair (figure 3.4).
- Roll the ball slightly forward, medially, or laterally to target various heads or areas of the muscle.
- If a trigger point or area of increased discomfort is found, stop rolling and target the area with constant pressure until the pain or soreness subsides or decreases.

Hamstring Release

Equipment

Trigger point stick and a bench

Starting Position

Sit on the edge of a bench with the whole hamstring off the bench. Place a trigger point stick under the back of the upper leg, and hold the handles with both hands.

Procedure

- Apply pressure upward into the hamstring. Roll the stick up and down the back of the leg from the knee to the butt.
- Focus attention on areas that feel knotted or are experiencing increased discomfort.

Tensor Fasciae Latae (TFL) Release

Equipment

Lacrosse ball or softball

Starting Position

Lie on one side rotated slightly forward with a ball just below the anterior superior iliac spine (ASIS), the front hip bone.

Procedure

- Roll up and down from the ASIS to just anterior to the greater trochanter (hip socket).
- If a trigger point or area of increased discomfort is found, stop rolling and target the area with constant pressure until the pain or soreness subsides or decreases.

Piriformis Release

Equipment

Lacrosse ball or softball

Starting Position

Lie on one side with the forearm and elbow on the floor. Place a ball behind the butt and roll back onto it at the level of the hip socket. The piriformis is located on a slight oblique angle, originating from the sacrum and connecting to the back of the greater trochanter.

Procedure

- Roll back and forth at a slight oblique angle from the sacrum to the greater trochanter.
- If a trigger point or area of increased discomfort is found, stop rolling and target the area with constant pressure until the pain or soreness subsides or decreases.

Note

The sciatic nerve is located under the piriformis muscle and sometimes becomes aggravated when the piriformis muscle is being released. If at any time numbness or tingling is felt in the area or in the same extremity, stop the release immediately. In most cases, just resting for a second and then reattempting the release will alleviate this sensation. If it persists, see a qualified message therapist, athletic trainer, or physical therapist to release the muscle.

Pec Release

Equipment

Lacrosse ball or softball

Starting Position

Stand facing a wall. Flex the elbow to 90 degrees; then abduct and externally rotate the shoulder until the elbow is at shoulder height and the forearm is parallel to the wall. Lean forward and pin a lacrosse ball between the pectoralis major muscle and the wall (figure 3.5). Female athletes may prefer to use a softball, whereas male athletes may prefer a lacrosse ball.

Procedure

- Roll back and forth at a slightly oblique angle from the sternum to the shoulder.
- If a trigger point or area of increased discomfort is found, stop rolling and target the area with constant pressure until the pain or soreness subsides or decreases.

Figure 3.5   Pec release; lacrosse ball between the pectoralis major and the wall.

Latissimus Dorsi and Teres Major Release

Equipment

Softball or lacrosse ball

Starting Position

Lie on one side with the bottom shoulder flexed and the elbow straight, placing the arm directly above the head. Place a ball under the posterior muscles that makes up the back of the armpit.

Procedure

- Rotate the body back and forth to apply pressure to the latissimus dorsi and teres major muscles that make up the back of the armpit.
- Then roll the ball up and down the side of the latissimus dorsi from the top of the armpit to the rib cage.
- If a trigger point or area of increased discomfort is found, stop rolling and target the area with constant pressure until the pain or soreness subsides or decreases.

Posterior Shoulder and Scapula Release

Equipment

Lacrosse ball

Starting Position

Lie supine on the floor. To work the posterior shoulder, place the lacrosse ball under the posterior shoulder just lateral to the scapula. To work the scapula (rotator cuff), place the lacrosse ball under the scapula.

Procedure

- These muscles are released by abducting and adducting the upper arm or rolling the ball around the scapula to release the infraspinatus and teres minor muscles.
- If a trigger point or area of increased discomfort is found, stop rolling and target the area with constant pressure until the pain or soreness subsides or decreases.

JOINT MOBILIZATION

Joint mobilizations (mobs) are exercises that increase range of motion in joints in specific planes of movement. Joint mobility is different from flexibility in that flexibility addresses the length of the muscle whereas joint mobility addresses the range of motion of the ligaments, fibrous capsules, musculature, and boney articulating surfaces that make up or cross the joint. Joint mobs tend to use movement instead of static holds (as in stretching) to promote proper joint mobility and function. While mobilizing a joint, the athlete may feel stiffness or tissue stretching, but the movement should always be pain free. A joint mob that causes pain should be stopped and not performed again until a medical professional has assessed the joint. Often, the term *translation* is used to describe a small motion into and then just back out of tension during a mobilization. This range of motion is small, and the movement is repeated without pauses.

Three-Plane Ankle Mob

Starting Position

Place hands on a wall at shoulder height with the feet 3 to 4 feet (1 to 1.2 m) from the wall, creating a straight line from the heels to the shoulders.

Procedure

This mob is performed in three planes of movement.
To work in the sagittal plane:

- Flex the left hip and knee until the thigh is perpendicular to the torso.
- Perform small translations, pushing the left knee toward and then away from the wall.
- When the knee moves toward the wall, the elbows should flex; when it moves away from the wall, the elbows should extend. This keeps the spine in a neutral position by maintaining a straight line from the heel to the shoulder.
- Keep the heel of the right foot flat on the floor and the toe pointed forward.

To work in the fontal plane:

- Reach the left foot to the left, anterior to the wall, and back to the start.
- Reach the left foot to the right, anterior to the wall, and back to the start.
- The combination of these movements resembles a V shape.
- When the foot moves toward the wall, the elbows should flex; when it moves away from the wall, the elbows should extend. This keeps the spine in a neutral position by maintaining a straight line from the heel to the shoulder.
- Throughout the mob, keep the right foot flat and toe pointed forward.

To work in the transverse plane:

- Flex the left hip and knee until the thigh is perpendicular to the torso.
- Push the left knee toward the wall and flex the arms at the elbows.
- Keeping the hip and knee flexed, perform leg swings from side to side with the left leg.

Standing Ankle Mob (Wall)

Equipment

Athletic or court tape and a marker

Setup

Place the tape on the floor against and perpendicular to the wall. Starting at the wall, mark lines at 1.5-centimeter (about 0.5 in.) increments to 15 centimeters (6 in.) on the tape.

Starting Position

Place the longest toe of the foot being mobilized toward the wall at the increment achieved during the ankle dorsiflexion test (see chapter 1).

Procedure

- Dorsiflex the ankle, moving the knee toward the wall while keeping the heel flat, the kneecap in line with the center toe, and the hips square to the wall.
- Hold at the end range of motion for a second, and then return to the starting position.
- If the knee touches the wall, move the heel away from the wall to work a greater range of motion.
- Repeat for the prescribed number of repetitions.

Note

The tape with 1.5-centimeter (0.5 in.) increments is the same scale used in the ankle dorsiflexion test in chapter 1. The tape is used in the mobilization exercise to provide an exact starting point, enable data to be recorded and progress to be tracked, and provide immediate feedback for motivation.

Half-Kneeling Ankle Mob

Equipment

Pad, dowel rod

Starting Position

Assume a half-kneeling position with one knee on a pad and the opposite leg flexed at the hip and knee and the foot flat on the floor. This creates a 90-degree angle with both legs. Hold a small dowel rod vertically from the floor just above the pinkie toe with the same hand as the leg that is forward.

Procedure

- Keeping the front foot flat and heel down, dorsiflex the ankle, pushing the knee both forward and lateral of the dowel rod (figure 3.6).
- Hold at the end range of motion for a second, and then return to the starting position.
- Repeat for the prescribed number of repetitions.

Variation

A heavy duty band can be used in combination with the mob to accentuate the roll, slide, glide effect of the tibia in relation to the talus bone. This is done by stepping the target ankle into a heavy-duty loop band anchored to a sturdy piece of equipment. Place the band around the ankle bone of the target leg and step out, stretching the band as much as possible. Perform the half kneeling ankle mob facing away from the anchor as directed in the main exercise.

Figure 3.6 Half-kneeling ankle mob; knee forward and lateral of the dowel rod.

▶ Shoulder Flexion Mob

Equipment

Pull-up bar

Starting Position

Stand with the feet hip-width apart. Grasp a pull-up bar or strap hanging from a pull-up bar overhead with the left hand, creating tension throughout the arm and shoulder.

Procedure

This mob is performed in three planes of movement. Small movements called *translations* are performed, moving the body in and out of tension driven by movements of the torso or hips.

- To work in the sagittal plane, perform small translation movements forward and back to the starting position with the hips and torso.

- To work in the frontal plane, perform small translation movements to the left and back to the starting position with the hips and torso.
- To work in the transverse plane, perform small translation movements rotating right with the hips and back to the starting position.
- To work in multiple planes, perform hip circles into tension to the right and left.

Seated Retract and Rotate Mob

Equipment

Bench, chair, or box

Starting Position

Sit upright on a bench, chair, or box. Bilaterally abduct the upper arms until the elbows are at shoulder height. Flex the elbows to 90 degrees and externally rotate the upper arms so the forearms are perpendicular to the floor. Then turn the hands so the thumbs are pointed back. Retract the head back and tuck the chin in.

Procedure

- Maximally retract the elbow and forearm (figure 3.7a).
- Maximally externally rotate the upper arm (figure 3.7b).

Figure 3.7   Seated retract and rotate mob: (a) maximally retract elbow and forearm; (b) maximally externally rotate upper arm.

- Once end range of motion is met, take one deep breath in and out and reset to the starting position.
- Repeat for the prescribed number of sets and repetitions.

Note

Make sure the movement occurs in the upper back and shoulder girdle, not the lumbar spine.

Thoracic Mob (Peanut)

Equipment

Peanut (two lacrosse balls taped together)

Starting Position

Lie supine on the floor, legs bent, and feet and low back flat on the floor with the peanut under the back just above the last rib. The arms are at the sides, elbows locked and knuckles pointing up.

Procedure

- Keeping the elbows locked, slowly move the arms into maximal shoulder flexion (figure 3.8), then back to the starting position.
- Try to squeeze the biceps toward the ears as the arms go past the head.
- Perform the prescribed number of repetitions, and then roll the peanut a half to full rotation toward the head.
- Repeat for the prescribed number of repetitions and positions.

Figure 3.8 Thoracic mob (peanut): *(a)* the peanut is placed behind the athlete's back; *(b)* the athlete lies on the peanut, moving the arms into maximal shoulder flexion.

Note

If desired, this exercise can be performed with a foam roller instead of a peanut.

Thoracic Mob (Foam Roll)

Equipment

4-inch (10 cm) foam roll

Starting Position

Lie supine on the floor with a foam roll under the back, perpendicular to the torso. The top of the foam roll should be positioned at the top of the shoulder blades. Interlock the fingers and rest the head in the hands. Make sure the entire body is relaxed. Legs and butt are on the floor, and arms and shoulder girdle are relaxed.

Procedure

- Take three to five deep breaths in and out, making sure to maximally expand the abdomen and rib cage, and then completely expel the air.
- After completing three to five breaths, roll the foam roll down the back a half or full rotation and perform another three to five breaths.
- Repeat for the prescribed positions, completing three to five breaths at each position.

Notes

- Breathing is key. It enhances relaxation, and the expanding and shrinking of the diaphragm and rib cage assist in mobilizing the thoracic spine.
- When performing five positions, move a half rotation of the foam roll per repetition; when performing three positions, perform a full rotation of the foam roll per repetition.

DYNAMIC STRETCHING

Dynamic stretching uses movement and momentum to increase mobility. The athlete performs a controlled movement to and then out of the end range of motion. It differs from static and ballistic stretching in that the stretch isn't held for an extended period of time and movements are performed in a controlled fashion, not with bouncing or jerking. Dynamic stretching is usually performed prior to training because it increases range of motion, increases blood flow to active muscles, can excite proprioceptors, and has no effect on power production.

▶ # Hand Walkout With Three-Plane Reach

Starting Position

Stand tall, feet under hips and toes pointed forward.

Procedure

- Keeping the knees straight, bend forward at the hips, reaching toward the floor.
- At the end range of motion of hip flexion (a feeling of tightening behind the knees or in the hamstrings may occur), round the back. If needed, bend the knees until the palms are on the floor.
- Hold this position for two deep breaths in and out.
- Walk the hands forward until they are 6 to 12 inches (15 to 30 cm) past the shoulders and the body forms a straight line from the ankles to the shoulders.
- Only moving at the ankles, walk the feet slowly toward the hands.
- With each step, drive the heel to the floor and briefly pause before the next foot takes a step.
- Perform ankle walks until the toes are just behind the palms or until the knees can no longer remain locked.
- Stand tall by extending the hips, knees, and trunk while flexing the upper arm at the shoulder and extending the elbows to reach as high as possible overhead.
- Drop the left arm down by your left side and reach the right arm overhead and to the left. Repeat on the other side by dropping your right arm down to the right side and reaching the left arm overhead and to the right.
- Reach the right arm across the body and over the left shoulder. Repeat on the other side by reaching the left arm across the body and over the right shoulder. To maximize the reach, follow your hand with your eyes.
- Repeat the sequence starting from the beginning.

Lunge and Twist

Starting Position

Stand tall with the feet under the hips and the toes pointing forward.

Procedure

- Flex the left knee and hip until the thigh is parallel to the floor and the upper and lower leg form a 90-degree angle.

- Step forward with the right foot and sink into a lunge position. In the lunge position, the right leg flexes at the hip and knee to create a 90-degree angle between the upper and lower leg. The right knee should be positioned directly above the right heel. The left leg should be slightly extended at the hip and flexed at the knee, creating an angle greater than 90 degrees. The torso should be vertical, with the shoulders directly over the hips.
- While in the lunge position, reach the right hand back toward the left heel and raise the left arm overhead (figure 3.9).

Figure 3.9   Lunge and twist: In lunge position, twist and reach the arm overhead.

- Hold this position for one deep breath in and out.
- Stand tall by extending the right hip and knee and flexing the left hip and knee until the left leg forms a 90-degree angle with the thigh parallel to the floor.
- Repeat, stepping forward with the right leg.

Notes

- Do not hold your breath during the exercise.
- Do not overextend the low back while reaching toward the back heel.
- Flex the hip and immediately step through to the next lunge instead of putting the foot down while transitioning from one leg to the other.

▶ Spiderman Crawl

Starting Position

Begin in a push-up position with the hands directly under the shoulders and the heels perpendicular to the floor.

Procedure

- Step forward with the left foot so that the left heel is under the left shoulder, the knee is over the arch of the foot, and the toe is pointed forward.

- Move the right hand 6 to 12 inches (15 to 30 cm) in front of the right shoulder.
- Relax the legs and hips so they drop toward the floor. Allow the left knee to drift to the outside.
- Push the chest toward the floor.
- Hold this position for two deep breaths in and out; then step forward with the right leg, keeping the hips close to the floor throughout the movement. Repeat with the right leg.

Note

In the desired range of motion, the shoulder blades should be below the front knee when pushing the chest to the floor.

Lateral Squat

Starting Position

Stand with the feet outside shoulder width and the toes pointed forward. Keeping the elbows straight, raise both arms up and out in front by flexing at the shoulders until the arms are parallel to the floor.

Procedure

- Squat, shifting the body weight to the right until the right thigh is parallel to the floor and the left leg is straight (figure 3.10).
- Both feet should remain flat on the floor, and the toes should point straight forward throughout the exercise.
- Pause at the bottom for a second, and then extend the right hip and knee and return to the starting position.

Figure 3.10   Lateral squat.

- Throughout the exercise, focus on keeping the shoulders back and the torso as upright as possible.
- Repeat, shifting the body weight to the left.

Notes

- The wider the stance is, the easier it is to keep the torso upright and achieve a full range of motion with the lower body. Athletes with mobility issues may need to start out with a wide stance and then work their feet closer together as they increase their range of motion.

- The lateral squat looks very similar to a side lunge. The difference is that in a lateral squat, the feet remain planted on the floor at all times. In a side lunge, the athlete takes a step while lunging to the side.

Cross Behind and Reach

Starting Position

Stand tall with the feet under the hips and the toes pointed forward.

Procedure

- Cross the right foot in front of the left foot.
- With the left arm, reach over the head and slightly to the right.
- Place the right arm on the right hip and apply pressure to sway the hips to the left (figure 3.11).
- Keep the left foot flat on the floor and the left knee straight.
- Hold for two deep breaths in and out before returning to the starting position.
- Repeat, crossing the left foot over the right and reaching the right arm overhead and to the left.

Figure 3.11 Cross behind and reach.

Wide Stance Groin

Starting Position

Position the feet in a very wide stance, toes facing forward or slightly in. Interlock the hands.

Procedure

In the sagittal plane:

- Straighten the arms at the elbows and reach up and over the head.

- Perform translation movements by reaching up and back over the head with the hands.
- Look at the hands as they move back (figure 3.12*a*) to maximize the range of motion.

In the frontal plane:

- Raise the arms overhead.
- Side bend and reach to the right with both arms (figure 3.12*b*), and then side bend and reach to the left with both arms.

In the transverse plane:

- Straighten the arms at the elbows and reach up and over the head.
- Perform movements in a V pattern, reaching over the right shoulder with both arms (figure 3.12*c*) and then over the left shoulder with both arms.

Figure 3.12   Wide stance groin: *(a)* sagittal plane, reaching over the head; *(b)* frontal plane, side bending to the right; *(c)* transverse plane, reaching over the right shoulder.

Box Hip Flexor 1 (Psoas)

Equipment

12 to 18-inch (30 to 46 cm) box

Starting Position

Stand facing the box with the left foot on the box and the right foot on the floor with the weight through the forefoot, heel in the air, and toes pointed forward. The left knee should be directly over the heel or slightly past the heel. Wrap the left thumb around the right thumb.

Procedure

This stretch is performed in three planes of movement. Small movements called *translations* are performed, moving the body in and out of tension driven by movements of the arms.

To work in the sagittal plane:

- Straighten the arms at the elbows and reach up and over the head (figure 3.13*a*).
- Perform translation movements by reaching up and back over the head with the hands.

To work in the frontal plane:

- Raise the arms overhead.
- Perform translation movements by reaching to the left with both arms and extending the right elbow (figure 3.13*b*).

To work in the transverse plane:

- Straighten the arms at the elbows and reach up and over the head.
- Perform translation movements by reaching over the left shoulder with both arms and extending the right elbow (figure 3.13*c*).

Figure 3.13   Box hip flexor 1 (psoas): *(a)* sagittal plane, reaching back over the head; *(b)* frontal plane, reaching to the left and extending the right elbow; *(c)* transverse plane, reaching over the left shoulder and extending the right elbow.

Box Hip Flexor 2 (Rectus Femoris)

Equipment

12- to 18-inch (30 to 16 cm) box

Starting Position

Stand facing away from the box with the right foot on the box, the weight on the forefoot, and the heel in the air. The left foot is flat on the floor, weight is evenly distributed throughout the whole foot, and the knee is bent and directly over the heel. Wrap the right thumb around the left thumb.

Procedure

This stretch is performed in three planes of movement. Small movements called *translations* are performed, moving the body in and out of tension driven by movements of the arms.

In the sagittal plane:

- Straighten the arms at the elbows and reach up and over the head.
- Perform translation movements by reaching up and back over the head with the hands (figure 3.14a).

In the frontal plane:

- Raise the arms overhead.
- Perform translation movements by reaching to the left with both arms and extending the right elbow (figure 3.14b).

In the transverse plane:

- Straighten the arms at the elbows and reach up and over the head.
- Perform translation movements by reaching over the left shoulder with both arms and extending the right elbow (figure 3.14c).

Figure 3.14   Box hip flexor 2 (rectus femoris): *(a)* sagittal plane, reaching back over the head; *(b)* frontal plane, reaching to the left and extending the right elbow; *(c)* transverse plane, reaching over the left shoulder and extending the right elbow.

TFL/IT Band

Equipment

12- to 18-inch (30 to 46 cm) box

Starting Position

Stand to the right side of the box with the right hip flexed and externally rotated, the knee bent, and the outside of the right foot on the box. The left foot is 2 to 3 feet (around 60 to 90 cm) from the box and flat on the floor, with the foot turned medially 15 to 25 degrees and the knee straight but not locked. Wrap the left thumb around the right thumb.

Procedure

This dynamic stretch is performed in three planes of movement. Small movements called *translations* are performed, moving the body in and out of tension driven by movements of the arms.

In the sagittal plane (arm driven):

- Straighten the arms at the elbows and reach up and over the head.
- Perform translation movements by reaching up and back over the head with the hands (figure 3.15a).

In the frontal plane (arm driven):

- Raise the arms overhead.
- Perform translation movements by reaching to the right with both arms and extending the left elbow (figure 3.15b).

In the transverse plane (arm driven):

- Straighten the arms at the elbows and reach up and over the head.
- Perform movements in a V pattern, reaching over the right shoulder with both arms (figure 3.15c) and then over the left shoulder.

Figure 3.15   TFL/IT band: (a) sagittal plane, reaching back over the head; (b) frontal plane, reaching to the right and extending the left elbow; (c) transverse plane, reaching over the right shoulder.

STRETCHING

Stretching is the act of lengthening a muscle or tendon to improve elasticity or tone. We use two types of stretching in our mobility program: static and proprioceptive neuromuscular facilitation (PNF).

In static stretching, an elongated muscle is held at the end range of motion for 30 seconds to 2 minutes. The stretch can be uncomfortable but should not be painful, and the range of motion should be gradually increased while the muscle slowly relaxes and lengthens.

PNF is a stretching technique that uses an isometric contraction followed by a passive stretch to facilitate a reflex relaxation or inhibition of the muscle to achieve greater range of motion. Although there are several PNF techniques, the contract-relax technique is highlighted in this chapter because of its versatility, productivity, and safety. This technique can be self-administered or performed with the assistance of a partner. In the PNF contract-relax technique, the athlete holds a passive stretch of the restricted muscle for 15 to 20 seconds. Next, she inhales and holds her breath while performing an isometric submaximal contraction with the target muscle for 3 to 5 seconds. Finally, she exhales and relaxes the target muscle and moves into a greater position of stretch. PNF is highly beneficial because good results can be achieved in a short period of time. Stretching may be uncomfortable but should never be painful. Stretching a muscle into pain can cause tissue injury.

Straight-Leg Calf Stretch

Equipment

Slant board or wall

Starting Position

Stand on one leg on a slant board, foot flat on the slant board and knee straight. If performing the stretch against a wall, stand with one foot wedged against the wall. The ball of the foot and the toes are on the wall, and the back of the heel is on the floor with the same knee locked out.

Procedure

- Keep the knee locked out and move the hips forward or toward the wall (figure 3.16).
- The kneecap should remain aligned with the center toe to prevent the arch of the foot from collapsing.
- Hold for the prescribed amount of time and then switch sides.

Figure 3.16   Straight-leg calf stretch.

Bent-Knee Calf Stretch

Equipment

Slant board or wall

Starting Position

Stand on one leg with the foot flat on the slant board. If performing the stretch against a wall, stand with one foot wedged against the wall. The ball of the foot and the toes are on the wall, and the back of the heel is on the floor.

Procedure

- Dorsiflex the ankle, moving the knee forward (figure 3.17).
- The kneecap should remain aligned with the center toe to prevent the arch of the foot from collapsing.
- Hold for the prescribed amount of time and then switch sides.

Figure 3.17 Bent-knee calf stretch.

Rectus Femoris Stretch

Equipment

Pad and stability ball

Starting Position

Get into a half-kneeling position with one knee on a pad. The other leg is flexed at the hip and knee, foot flat on the floor and forming a 90-degree angle. Place the top of the foot of the kneeling leg on a stability ball.

Procedure

- Posteriorly rotate the hips by contracting the glute on the side of the kneeling leg (figure 3.18a). This could be an adequate stretch if the rectus femoris is tight.
- To increase the stretch, reach the arm on the same side as the kneeling leg over the head and slightly to the side (figure 3.18b).

Figure 3.18　Rectus femoris stretch: *(a)* rotate the hips; *(b)* increase the stretch by reaching the arm overhead and to the side.

IT Band Stretch

Equipment

Wall

Starting Position

Stand perpendicular to and 12 to 18 inches (30 to 46 cm) from a wall. Place the forearm on the wall with the elbow straight out from the shoulder and the hand perpendicular to the torso. Take the outside leg and step over and across the inside leg. Take the hand that is away from the wall and place it on the hip bone that is away from the wall.

Figure 3.19　IT band stretch.

Procedure

- Apply pressure with the hand into the hip, pushing the pelvis toward the wall (figure 3.19).
- Keep the upper arm of the arm on the wall perpendicular to the wall. This creates a bowing or lateral bend at the pelvis.
- You may have to rotate the hip closer to the wall forward or back to place the IT band right over the greater trochanter of the femur.

Note

The leg being stretched is the leg closer to the wall before performing the crossover step. This leg should remain straight but not locked out throughout the stretch.

Supine Hamstring Stretch

Equipment

Band or strap

Starting Position

Lie supine on the floor. Place the band or strap around the foot and hold the ends in both hands.

Procedure

- Flex the quad, locking the knee.
- Keeping the knee locked, pull the leg up with the band or strap so the foot moves toward the head (figure 3.20).
- Stop and hold when a moderate stretch is felt in the back of the leg.

Figure 3.20   Supine hamstring stretch.

Half-Kneeling Psoas Stretch With Band

Equipment

Pad and heavy-duty loop band

Starting Position

Anchor a heavy-duty band to a wall or machine. Facing the anchor, step one leg into the band, kneel down, and pull the band around the back of the upper thigh just under the glute. Move back to increase tension on the band. Get into a half-kneeling position with the involved leg's knee on the pad and the opposite leg flexed at the hip and the knee and foot on the floor, creating a 90-degree angle.

Procedure

- Rotate the hips posteriorly and squeeze the glute on same side as the kneeling leg.
- Reach up as high as possible with the same arm as the leg that is kneeling (figure 3.21).
- Kneel tall, but make sure not to arch at the low back.
- Hold for the prescribed amount of timed and then switch sides.

Note

This stretch can be enhanced by using up to three leg positions. The hip can be in neutral, laterally rotated 5 to 10 degrees, or slightly rotated 10 to 15 degrees. In a half-kneeling position, the lateral rotation of the hip causes the lower leg to move toward the midline of the body.

Figure 3.21   Half-kneeling psoas stretch with band.

Three-Position Groin Rock

Equipment

Volleyball knee pads or two pads

Starting Position

Get in a four-point position, kneeling on both knees with the forearms resting on the floor. In this position, abduct the legs maximally, pulling the knees away from each other.

Procedure

This exercise is performed in three positions: heels outside the knees (figure 3.22a), heels even with the knees (figure 3.22b), and heels inside the knees (figure 3.22c).

- Rock the hips back, keeping the torso parallel to the floor.
- Hold for the prescribed repetitions and time

Figure 3.22 Three-position groin rock: *(a)* heels outside knees; *(b)* heels even with knees; *(c)* heels inside knees.

PNF Standing Piriformis Stretch

Equipment

Table or tall plyometric box and multiple pads

Starting Position

Stand facing a table. Flex and externally rotate the hip and flex the knee so the leg makes a 90-degree angle with the torso and at the knee. Place the lower leg, knee, and lower third of the femur on the table.

Procedure

- Place the hand that is on the same side as the leg on the table on the involved knee and apply pressure, pushing the knee to the table.
- Stand tall, push the butt back, and hinge forward at the hip (figure 3.23).
- To increase the stretch, bend the knee of the leg you're standing on.
- Perform in three positions: sternum pointing toward knee, sternum pointing toward midshin, and sternum pointing toward heel.
- Hold for the prescribed sets and time

Figure 3.23   PNF standing piriformis stretch.

Notes

- If the table or box is not high enough to elicit a good stretch, place pads on the table to increase the height.
- If a pain or ache is felt on the outside of the involved knee, place another pad under the knee for support.

Forearm to Instep Complex

Equipment

Pad

Starting Position

Place the right knee on the pad. Flex the left hip and knee, placing the left foot forward so the knee is over the arch of the foot. Lean forward and grasp the left foot with the right hand. Place the right forearm on the floor even with the arch of the left foot. Take the left hand and grab the left foot or ankle.

Procedure

- Keeping the foot flat on the floor, push the left knee laterally with the left elbow and drive the chest to the ankle. Hold for 20 seconds.
- Reposition the torso so the sternum is facing the middle of the left shin; then repeat, pushing the left knee laterally and this time driving the sternum toward the shin. Hold for 20 seconds.
- Reposition the torso so the sternum is facing the left knee and repeat, pushing the left knee laterally and driving the sternum to the knee. Hold for 20 seconds.
- Move the right forearm off the floor and place the right hand out in front of the right foot. Take the left arm and flex it at the elbow, creating a 90-degree angle. Flex the right elbow and drive the left elbow toward the floor. Hold for 20 seconds.
- Repeat on the opposite side.

Note

If you are not flexible enough to place the forearm on the floor, put one or more pads under the forearm to match the range of motion.

PNF Supine Hip Flexion (Band)

Equipment

Heavy band

Setup

Anchor a heavy-duty loop band to a sturdy piece of equipment.

Starting Position

Sit on the floor and place the right leg inside the band and pull it over the knee. Flex the hip and knee and place the band around the upper thigh just beneath the pelvis (figure 3.24a).

Procedure

- Pull the right knee to the chest and extend the left leg, pushing the body away from the anchor of the band, thereby increasing the resistance of the band (figure 3.24b).
- Hold for the prescribed sets and time

Figure 3.24   PNF supine hip flexion: (a) starting position; (b) pulling right knee to chest and extending left leg.

PNF Standing Shoulder Flexion (Band)

Equipment

Medium-duty loop band

Setup

Attach the band to the top of a squat rack or pull-up bar.

Starting Position

Place one hand inside the band with the palm facing up.

Procedure

- Bend the knees slightly and flex forward at the trunk so the shoulder moves into flexion (figure 3.25).
- Hold the position for 15 seconds.
- Take a deep breath and hold the breath.

Figure 3.25   PNF standing shoulder flexion.

- Retract the head of the humerus to the back of its socket, lock the elbow, and then extend at the shoulder creating tension in the band.
- Hold the contraction for 3 seconds.
- Exhale, relax, and move further into the stretch for another 15 seconds.
- Repeat.
- After a couple of PNF segments, move the feet, rotate, or side bend the torso to pinpoint the plane in which the shoulder is most restricted.
- Repeat PNF.

Internal Shoulder Rotator Stretch

Starting Position

Stand so the toes are behind a doorway, the corner of a wall, or the side of a squat rack. Abduct and externally rotate the shoulder and flex the elbow so the upper arm is parallel to the floor and the lower arm is perpendicular to the floor and bent at 90 degrees. Place the hand, forearm, and elbow on the doorway, wall, or rack.

Procedure

- Keeping the back in neutral, flex forward at the hips until tension is felt in the front of the shoulder (figure 3.26).
- Hold for the prescribed amount of time.

Notes

- The muscles of the rotator cuff are small and should be stretched only to a point of mild discomfort.
- PNF can be performed, creating an isometric hold by internally rotating the shoulder, applying pressure through the hand into the wall.

Figure 3.26   Internal shoulder rotator stretch.

Sleeper Stretch

Starting Position

Lie on the right side with the right shoulder abducted and the elbow flexed to 90 degrees. The elbow should be straight out from the shoulder, and the lower arm should be perpendicular to the floor.

Procedure

- Take the left arm and apply pressure on the right wrist, internally rotating the shoulder and pushing the hand toward the floor (figure 3.27).
- Rotate the shoulder to the point of mild tension. If this tension dissipates, move further into the stretch.

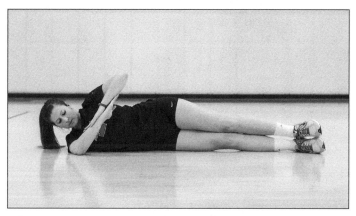

Figure 3.27   Sleeper stretch.

Notes

- The muscles of the rotator cuff are small and should be stretched only to the point of mild discomfort.
- PNF stretching can be performed by executing an isometric contraction. Externally rotate the right arm while resisting with the left hand; then relax further into the stretch.

External Shoulder Rotator Stretch: Behind the Back

Starting Position

Stand tall facing away from a doorjamb. Retract the right shoulder blade toward the spine. Reach behind the back with the right hand and grasp the doorjamb with the thumb pointed up.

Procedure

Figure 3.28   External shoulder rotator stretch: behind the back.

- Keeping the shoulder blade retracted and pulled toward the spine, walk the fingers up the doorjamb until a stretch is felt in the back of the shoulder (figure 3.28).
- If a stretch isn't felt, bend the knees to increase tension on the shoulder.

SUMMARY

Mobility is the foundation to optimizing athletic potential and reducing injuries. Improvements of marked restrictions in movements or joints should be a high priority to prevent plateaus in training and reduce the likelihood of injury.

Chapter 4

Balance and Stability

Balance and stability are prerequisites to all other components of training. Joint stability while in motion is essential to maintain efficient joint alignment; to produce a solid platform to generate force, power, and speed; and to prevent injury. A single-leg stance stresses balance and activates the smaller muscles of the hip, ankle, and foot that are not normally stimulated in a bilateral stance.

Unilateral movements are prevalent throughout the game of volleyball. Some examples are jumping off one leg such as in the slide attack and accelerating or changing direction to make a play on defense. Also, although it is not correct technique, some volleyball players land on one leg after an attack or make plays with most of their weight on one leg. Because of the many occurrences of unilateral movements on the court, training must involve single-leg power production and eccentric deceleration (landing and cutting) in multiple planes of movement.

The following exercises focus on building strength and stability as the athlete moves through multiple planes of movement, or on teaching the body to decelerate movement in the frontal or transverse planes.

Toe Touch to Balance

Purpose

To increase lower-body joint stability in multiple planes with movement initiated by the lower body (foot)

Starting Position

Balance on the left leg. After completing all three parts on the left leg, repeat while balancing on the right leg.

Part 1

- Reach the right foot forward as far as possible, lightly touching the toes to the floor (figure 4.1*a*). Return to the starting position.
- Reach the right foot as far back as possible, lightly touching the toes to the floor (figure 4.1*b*). Return to the starting position.
- Throughout the exercise keep the shoulders over the hips and the right heel on the floor.
- As you go through the repetitions, try to increase the reach distance. Make the transition from forward to back smooth and integrated, and increase the speed of movement.
- After completing the prescribed number of touches, perform the same movements without touching the toes to the floor.

Part 2

- Reach the right foot as far right as possible, lightly touching the toes to the floor (figure 4.2*a*). Return to the starting position.
- Keeping the toe pointed forward, reach the right foot over the left foot as far left as possible, lightly touching the toes to the floor (figure 4.2*b*). Return to the starting position.
- Throughout the exercise keep the shoulders over the hips and the right foot flat on the floor.
- As you go through the repetitions, try to increase the reach distance. Make the transition from forward to back smooth and integrated, and increase the speed of movement.
- After completing the prescribed number of touches, perform the same movements without touching the toes to the floor.

Figure 4.1 Toe touch to balance, part 1: *(a)* reach right foot forward; *(b)* reach right foot back.

Figure 4.2 Toe touch to balance, part 2: *(a)* reach right foot to the right; *(b)* reach right foot to the left.

Part 3

- Open the hips by rotating to the right and reaching the right foot as far back as possible, lightly touching the toes to the floor (figure 4.3a). Return to the starting position. Close the hips by rotating to the left and reaching the right foot as far to the left as possible, lightly touching the toes to the floor (figure 4.3b). Return to the starting position.
- Throughout the exercise keep the shoulders over the hips and the right foot flat on the floor.
- As you go through the repetitions, try to increase the distance you touch. Make the transition from forward to back smooth and integrated, and increase the speed of movement.
- After completing the prescribed number of touches, perform the same movements without touching the toes to the floor.

Figure 4.3   Toe touch to balance, part 3: (a) open hips and reach right foot back; (b) close hips and reach right foot to the left.

▶ Matrix Reaches

Purpose

To increase lower-body joint stability in multiple planes with movement initiated by the upper body (hand)

Starting Position

Balance on the left leg.

Procedure

- Rotate to the left and reach and touch the floor behind the left heel with the right hand. Return to the starting position.
- Reach with both hands and touch the floor as far forward as possible while keeping the left heel on the floor. Return to the starting position.
- Open the hips by rotating to the right, touching the floor behind the left heel with the left hand. Return to the starting position.
- Repeat for the prescribed number of repetitions. Then perform while balancing on the right leg.

Note

On returning to the starting position, stand tall, maximally extending both the hip and the knee. If you are double jointed, do not hyperextend the knee; rather, return to a straight-leg position.

▶ Single-Leg Squat

Purpose

To develop single-leg strength and stability in a squat pattern

Equipment

6-inch and 12-inch (15 and 30 cm) plyometric boxes and multiple 1- and 2-inch (2.5 and 5 cm) pads

Starting Position

Facing away from the plyometric box, balance on the left leg with the left heel 2 inches (5 cm) from the box.

Procedure

- Keeping the torso as vertical as possible and the knee aligned with the foot and hip, squat down until the butt lightly touches the box.
- During the squat, bring the arms up from the sides and hold them straight out in front to help counterbalance the body.
- Pause at the box, but do not transfer any weight onto the box.
- Return to the starting position, standing tall between repetitions.

Note

Depending on your height, mobility, balance, and strength, you may have to start at a different height box. The goal of the exercise is to gradually decrease the height of the box and increase the exercise range of motion through various combinations of boxes and pads. Once you can achieve a depth with the thigh slightly below parallel to the floor, add more weight by holding a weight plate against the chest or a bar in a front squat position.

Single-Arm, Single-Leg RDL

Purpose

To develop single-leg stability and strength. The primary muscles creating movement are the glutes and the hamstrings. Unilateral loading with a weight in the hand opposite the balance leg increases muscle recruitment in the obliques, the lateral hip, and the muscles crossing the ankle joint and the foot.

Equipment

Kettlebell or dumbbell

Starting Position

Stand on the left leg, holding a kettlebell in the right hand. Pull the right scapula back toward the spine.

Procedure

- Squat down slightly through the left hip and knee (figure 4.4a).
- The knee should be bent at least 15 degrees to activate the gluteus maximus.
- Flex forward at the hip, keeping the lumbar spine and pelvis neutral until the hand reaches midshin level (figure 4.4b).

Figure 4.4   Single-arm, single-leg RDL: (a) squat slightly; (b) flex forward at the hip.

- The range of motion may be shorter if a stretch is felt in the hamstring or if maintaining a neutral lumbar spine is not possible.
- Return to the starting position by extending the hip and knee, standing tall and squeezing the glute.
- Repeat on the right leg, holding the weight in the left arm.

Note

The goal of this exercise is to generate all the movement through the hip. If the athlete goes past the available hip range of motion, the coach will see one or a combination of the lumbar spine flexing, the knee moving forward or backward, or the pelvis rotating away from the balance leg.

▶ Single-Arm, Single-Leg Deadlift

Purpose

To develop single-leg stability and strength. The primary muscles creating movement are the glutes and the hamstrings. Unilateral loading with a weight in the hand opposite the balance leg increases muscle recruitment in the obliques, the lateral hip, and the muscles crossing the ankle joint and the foot.

Equipment

Kettlebell or dumbbell

Starting Position

Stand on the left leg, holding a kettlebell in the right hand. Pull the right scapula back toward the spine.

Procedure

- Squat down slightly through the left hip and knee.
- The knee should be bent at least 15 degrees to activate the gluteus maximus.
- Flex forward at the hip, keeping the lumbar spine and pelvis neutral until the weight or hand gets to the kneecap.
- Squat down 2 to 6 inches (5 to 15 cm) through the hip, not changing the angle of the back.
- Return to the starting position by standing up out of the squat until the kettlebell passes the knee and then extending the hip. Stand tall and squeeze the butt. Repeat, balancing on the right leg and holding the weight in the left hand.

Single-Leg RDL

Purpose

To increase single-leg stance stability and improve force production of the posterior chain. The primary muscles are the glutes and hamstrings.

Equipment

Barbell

Starting Position

Stand tall, balancing on the left leg and holding a barbell in a shoulder-width grip with shoulder blades retracted and elbows straight.

Procedure

- Squat down slightly through the hips and knees (figure 4.5a).
- The knee should be bent at least 15 degrees to activate the gluteus maximus.
- Flex forward at the hip, keeping the lumbar spine and pelvis neutral until the bar reaches midshin level (figure 4.5b).
- The range of motion may be shorter if a stretch is felt in the hamstring or if maintaining a neutral lumbar spine is not possible. Return to the starting position by bringing the hips forward toward the bar, extending the hip and knee, standing tall, and squeezing the glute.

Figure 4.5 Single-leg RDL: (a) holding barbell, squat slightly; (b) flex forward through hips, keeping back and pelvis neutral.

Note

The goal of this exercise is to generate all the movement through the hip. If the athlete goes past her available hip range of motion, the coach will see the lumbar spine flexing, the knee moving forward or backward, or a combination of these.

▶ Single-Leg Deadlift

Purpose

To develop single-leg stability and force production of the posterior chain. The primary muscles are the glutes and hamstrings.

Equipment

Barbell

Starting Position

Stand tall, balancing on the left leg and holding a barbell in a shoulder-width grip with shoulder blades retracted and elbows straight.

Procedure

- Squat down slightly through the hips and knees.
- The knee should be bent at least 15 degrees to activate the gluteus maximus.
- Flex forward through the hips while keeping the back and pelvis in neutral until the bar passes the kneecap.
- Squat down 2 to 6 inches (5 to 15 cm) through the hip, not changing the angle of the back.
- Return to the starting position by standing up out of the squat until the bar passes the knee. Then extend the hip to the bar, stand tall, and squeeze the butt.

▶ Walking Lunge With Medicine Ball Arc

Purpose

To develop strength and stability in a lunge pattern

Equipment

Medicine ball or weight plate

Procedure: Forward Walking Lunge

- Stand tall, holding a medicine ball or weight plate with two hands positioned on the right side of the right hip.
- Lunge forward by flexing the hip and knee of the right leg while simultaneously lifting the medicine ball or weight plate from the right hip in an arcing motion over the head and to the left hip.
- Repeat, lunging forward with the left leg and arcing the medicine ball or weight plate overhead back to the right hip.
- Repeat, moving forward for the prescribed number of repetitions; then perform the same motion in a backward lunge.

Procedure: Backward Walking Lunge

- Start in a lunge position with the left foot forward and the right foot back, holding the medicine ball or weight plate at the right hip.
- Lunge backward with the left leg and move the medicine ball or weight plate in an arcing motion over the head and to the left hip.
- Repeat, lunging back with the right leg and arcing the medicine ball or plate overhead to the right hip.

Notes

- When transitioning lunges from leg to leg, do not put the foot down in the middle.
- To increase difficulty, increase the rate at which the plate moves from side to side. The faster the plate moves, the harder it is to maintain balance.

Single-Arm, Single-Leg Cable Row

Purpose

To develop total-body joint stability and balance while training a rowing pattern. The primary muscles creating motion are the scapular abductors, rear deltoids, and biceps.

Equipment

Cable machine

Setup

Set the handle of the cable machine at the low position.

Starting Position

Face the cable machine from 3 to 4 feet (1 to 1.2 m) away. Balance on the left leg, knee slightly bent and hip flexed forward, holding the cable handle in the right hand (figure 4.6a).

Procedure

- Row the handle as far into the right armpit as possible (figure 4.6*b*). Return to the starting position.
- Throughout the exercise, keep the knee aligned with the hip and foot and the pelvis square to the cable machine.
- Repeat, balancing on the right foot and holding the cable handle in the left hand.

Figure 4.6 Single-arm, single-leg cable row: *(a)* starting position; *(b)* rowing the handle to the right armpit.

Single-Arm Cable Push

Purpose

To develop pelvic and spinal segmental stability while performing sagittal plane pressing. The primary muscles creating motion are the pectoralis major, anterior deltoid, and triceps.

Equipment

Cable machine

Setup

Position the cable machine handle between the hip and the shoulder.

Starting Position

Standing 3 to 4 feet (1 to 1.2 m) away, face away from the cable machine in a split stance with the right foot forward and the left foot back. Hold the handle of the cable machine in the left hand with the left elbow at shoulder height, the elbow bent at 90 degrees, and the forearm parallel to the floor (figure 4.7*a*).

Procedure

- Press the cable out in front, extending the elbow (figure 4.7*b*). Return to the starting position.
- Throughout the exercise, keep the shoulders and hips facing forward and move only through the arm.

Figure 4.7　Single-arm cable push: *(a)* starting position; *(b)* pressing the cable out in front.

SUMMARY

Training for balance and stability is essential to maximize strength, power, and movement efficiency. It also can reduce the chance for injury. Training must consist of single-leg multiplane movement or stabilizing against multiplane movement to prepare athletes for the demands of the game of volleyball.

Chapter 5

Strength

Strength training is critical to the physical development of the volleyball athlete. The main focus should be on maximal force production. The strength program needs to include bilateral and unilateral stance exercises performed in multiple planes of movement. Free weights are used instead of machines to allow freedom of movement, promote joint stability, and train functionally in an upright standing position. The benefits of strength training include an increase in neuromuscular efficiency, muscle size, connective tissue tensile strength, and bone density. This chapter explains the strength/power relationship, the need for a strength base, and training for strength and presents exercises to improve strength.

STRENGTH/POWER RELATIONSHIP

The ultimate goal in volleyball performance training is to increase power production. The role of strength training in force production and its effect on power output is best explained by analyzing the equations for power and force:

Power = force × velocity

Force = mass × acceleration

Force and velocity are the two components that make up power. If either of these increases, power increases. Developing a base of strength is crucial because of the effect of gravity on the body and the need to produce ground reaction forces to resist it. From a stationary position, an athlete trying to accelerate, whether linearly, horizontally, or vertically (such as when sprinting or jumping), must create force into the ground to overcome gravity. The greater the force displaced into the ground, the faster the athlete accelerates in the opposite direction. Basically, if an athlete's ability to generate force increases but her body weight remains the same, she will jump higher as a result of an increased capacity to accelerate her own mass.

Without a base of strength to create force into the ground and overcome gravity, athletes cannot achieve maximal velocity. Essentially, they can train the neuromuscular system to perform quicker, more explosive movements, as in power training and plyometrics, but if they do not have the strength to produce force, they will obtain only minimal gains in jumping, accelerating, decelerating, and changing direction.

STRENGTH BASE

How much strength is enough? When an athlete first begins strength training, he will see significant increases in power as his ability to generate force increases. As strength gains rise over time, the benefits become less pronounced. Larger gains in strength are needed to elicit the same gain in power. As force production increases, so does the weight or load needed to stimulate the body to adapt and get stronger. At some point the load that the athlete must lift to gain a slight increase in power is outweighed by the higher potential for injury. This line of risk and reward is different for each person and is based on medical history, current physical state, and body type. As a general rule, for a solid base of lower-body strength, women should back squat 1 to 1.5 times their body weight (1RM) and men should back squat 1.5 to 2 times their body weight (1RM). Without a base of strength to create force into the ground, overcome gravity, and create momentum, maximal velocity will not be obtained. As with the strength/power relationship, athletes can train their neuromuscular systems to perform quicker, more explosive movements, as in Olympic lifts and plyometrics, but if they do not have the strength to produce force, they will obtain only minimal gains in jumping, accelerating, decelerating, and changing direction.

TRAINING FOR STRENGTH

Athletes must work at a high intensity to maximize force development—that is, a high percentage of the 1-repetition maximum (1RM). A 1RM is the amount of weight a person can lift with proper technique for just one repetition. When executing strength exercises for maximal force production, athletes should perform between three and five repetitions in most sets. Ranges of 8 to 10 repetitions with lower weights are used in the beginning of the training phase to learn or refresh technique and to progressively increase the load on the body. Ranges of one or two repetitions are not usually performed within a work set because of the high load, the difficulty in executing technique properly, and the higher potential for injury.

During the lift, the eccentric phase (loading of the muscle) should be controlled and the concentric movement should be performed with the intent to move the weight as fast as possible. *Intent* is the key word here because with a heavy weight the actual speed of the concentric contraction will not be fast throughout the full range of motion. The intent alone has shown to increase muscle motor unit recruitment as well as stress the component of all-out effort needed to maximize the velocity component during the lift. Therefore, repetition ranges of three to five will help facilitate maximal force production.

▶ Back Squat

Purpose

To develop lower-body force production by strengthening the hips and thighs

Equipment

Squat rack, barbell, weight plates

Starting Position

- Grip the bar with a closed, pronated grip, hands slightly outside shoulder width.
- Step under the center of the bar and place it on the upper trapezius, right on top of the shoulder blades.
- Pull the elbows down and back and squeeze the shoulder blades together to form a shelf for the bar to rest on.
- Extend the hips and knees to lift the bar off the rack, and take one or two small steps back.
- Make sure the feet are parallel and slightly outside shoulder width and that the toes point slightly out.
- The low back should be in a neutral position.

Descent

- Before lowering into the squat, inhale and hold your breath.
- Initiate the movement by dropping the butt down, flexing at both the hips and knees.
- Keep the feet flat on the floor with an even weight distribution between the heels and the forefeet.
- The knees should remain aligned over the feet.
- The low back should remain in neutral.

- The torso will slightly flex forward as a result of the bar position.
- Continue the descent until the pelvis begins to posteriorly rotate (hips rotating underneath) or the upper thighs are parallel to the floor.

Ascent

- The upward movement should be performed with the intent to move the bar as explosively and rapidly as possible. The word *intent* is used because you may exert an effort to move the bar fast, but because of the load, the ascent may be gradual.
- Extend the hips and knees, driving out of the bottom of the squat to the starting position.
- Exhale the held breath through pursed lips during the last third of the ascent.
- Maintain a neutral spine and rigid torso throughout the upward movement.
- Keep the feet flat, the weight evenly distributed between the heels and forefeet, and the knees aligned over the feet.

▶ Front Squat

Purpose

To increase lower-body force production and trunk stability. The front squat strengthens both the hips and thighs but is more quad dominant than the back squat.

Equipment

Squat rack, barbell, weight plates

Starting Position

- Step under the bar and place the barbell on the anterior deltoids (anterior shoulder).
- Elevate the elbows so the arms are parallel to the floor.
- Bend at both elbows, crisscrossing the arms and placing the hands on top of the barbell.
- Extend the hips and knees to lift the bar off the rack, and take one or two small steps back away from the squat rack after securing the barbell.
- Make sure the feet are parallel and shoulder-width apart or slightly outside shoulder width, and that the toes point slightly out.
- The low back should be in a neutral position.

Descent

- Before lowering into the squat, inhale and hold your breath.
- Initiate the movement by dropping the butt down, flexing at both the hips and knees.
- Keep the feet flat on the floor with an even weight distribution between the heels and the forefeet.
- The knees should remain aligned over the feet.
- The low back should remain in neutral.
- During the descent, keep the upper arms parallel to the floor and the torso as vertical as possible.
- Continue the descent until the pelvis begins to posteriorly rotate (hips rotating underneath) or the upper thighs are parallel to the ground.

Ascent

- The upward movement should be performed with the intent to move the bar as explosively and rapidly as possible. The word *intent* is used because you may exert an effort to move the bar fast, but because of the load, the ascent may be gradual.
- Extend the hips and knees, driving out of the bottom of the squat to the starting position.
- Exhale the held breath through pursed lips during the last third of the ascent.
- Maintain a neutral spine and rigid torso throughout the upward movement.
- Keep the feet flat, the weight evenly distributed between the heels and forefeet, and the knees aligned over the feet.

Three-Way Lunge

Purpose

To strengthen the hips and thighs in a lunging pattern in multiple planes of movement

Equipment

Sandbag, weight vest, or dumbbells

Starting Position

If using a sandbag, stand tall while holding it on the anterior deltoids. With dumbbells, stand tall while holding a single dumbbell at the chest with the handle vertical and the palms of both hands under the circular portion of the weight. If using a weight vest, make sure to secure it firmly and keep the shoulders over the hips throughout the movement.

Part 1: Forward Lunge

- With the left leg, take a long stride forward.
- Drop straight down by flexing the hips and the knee of the front leg and flexing the knee of the back leg until it is just off the floor (figure 5.1*a*).
- The left knee should be directly over the left heel.
- Maintain an equal weight distribution between the front and back legs and in the heel and forefoot of the left foot.
- Keep the shoulders over the hips.
- Pause at the bottom; then explosively push through the front foot, extending the left hip, knee, and ankle to get back to the starting position.
- Repeat with the right leg lunging forward.

Part 2: Lateral Lunge

- With the left foot, take a big step to the left.
- Drop down by flexing the left hip and knee (figure 5.1*b*). Keep the torso as vertical as possible.
- Keep both feet flat.
- The left foot should have equal weight distribution between the heel and forefoot.
- The right knee should remain straight but not locked out.
- Pause at the bottom and explosively push through the left foot, extending the left hip, knee, and ankle to get back to the starting position.
- Repeat, lunging to the right with the right foot.

Part 3: Pivot Lunge

- Keep the right foot pointing forward.
- Step back and laterally, putting the left foot perpendicular to the right.
- Drop down, flexing the left hip and knee and keeping the torso as vertical as possible (figure 5.1*c*).
- Keep both feet flat.
- The left foot should have equal weight distribution between the heel and forefoot.
- The right knee should be slightly bent.

- Pause at the bottom and push explosively through the left foot, extending the left hip, knee, and ankle to get back to the starting position.
- Repeat, lunging with the right foot.

Figure 5.1   Three-way lunge: *(a)* forward lunge; *(b)* lateral lunge; *(c)* pivot lunge.

Forward and Lateral Lunge

Purpose

To develop sagittal and frontal plane lower-body strength. The primary muscle groups involved are the quadriceps, hamstrings, glutes, and adductors.

Equipment

Squat rack, barbell, weight plates

Starting Position

- Grip the barbell with a closed, pronated grip, hands slightly wider than shoulder width.
- Step under the center of the bar and place it on the upper trapezius, right on top of the shoulder blades.
- Pull the elbows down and back and squeeze the shoulder blades together to form a shelf for the bar to rest on.
- Step out of the rack with the bar and stand upright with the feet directly under the hips.

Forward Lunge

- Step forward with the left leg and sink into a lunge by flexing the left hip and flexing the right knee until it is just above the floor (figure 5.2a).
- Return to the starting position by pushing off the left foot and extending the ankle, knee, and hip.
- Keep the shoulders over the hips throughout the exercise.

Lateral Lunge

- Step to the left and flex the left hip and knee (figure 5.2b).
- Keep the right leg straight but not locked out and both feet flat on the floor.
- Pause at the bottom; then quickly extend the left hip, knee, and ankle to get back to the starting position.

Figure 5.2 Forward and lateral lunge: (a) forward lunge; (b) lateral lunge.

▶ Box Step-Up

Purpose

To increase unilateral force production in the lower body. This drill strengthens both the hips and thighs.

Equipment

Sturdy step-up box, squat rack, barbell, weight plates

Starting Position

- Grip the bar with a closed, pronated grip, hands slightly wider than shoulder width.
- Step under the center of the bar and place it on the upper trapezius, right on top of the shoulder blades.
- Pull the elbows down and back and squeeze the shoulder blades together to form a shelf for the bar to rest on.
- Step out of the rack with the bar and stand in front of the box.
- Place the whole left foot on the box, creating a 90-degree angle between the lower and upper leg.

Ascent

- Extend the left hip and knee while simultaneously flexing the right hip and knee.
- The knee drive of the right leg creates momentum and assists in extending the left hip.
- The left foot should remain flat on the box, and the knee should remain aligned with the foot and hip.
- Keep the torso upright throughout the exercise.

Descent

- Slowly flex the left hip and knee and reach the right foot toward the floor.
- The descent should be slow and controlled with the left foot flat on the box and the left knee aligned with the hip and foot.

Chin-Up/Pull-Up

Purpose

To develop strength in the upper back with emphasis on the latissimus dorsi and biceps

Note

Because of the muscle's anterior insertion on the humerus, the latissimus dorsi internally rotates the upper arm. In a shortened state, the latissimus dorsi, like the chest muscles, can cause an internally rotated posture of the humerus. Weekly volume of scapular abduction should match or exceed the volume of both pressing and pull-up/chin-up sets combined.

Equipment

Pull-up bar or heavy weight bands if you can't do a full-range-of-motion body-weight pull-up

Starting Position

- Chin-up (figure 5.3): Hang from a bar using a supine grip, arms and elbows straight.
- Pull-up (figure 5.4): Hang from a bar using a prone grip, arms and elbows straight.

Procedure

- Extend the shoulder and flex the elbow until the chin passes the bar.
- Lower yourself under control back to the starting position.

Variation

If you cannot perform a body-weight chin-up or pull-up, use a heavy-, medium-, or light-duty loop band to assist with the chin-up or pull-up and allow a full range of motion throughout the exercise. This is done by hanging the band from the pull-up bar and inserting one knee into the loop. The tension of the band helps lift you so you can perform a full chin-up or pull-up. As you get stronger, switch to a lighter band until no band is needed.

Figure 5.3   Chin-up: *(a)* starting position; *(b)* chin passes the bar.

Figure 5.4   Pull-up: *(a)* starting position; *(b)* chin passes the bar.

Standing Lat Pull-Down

Purpose

To strengthen shoulder flexion and develop core stability

Equipment

Cable machine

Setup

Attach a straight bar at the high position on a cable column.

Starting Position

- Grasp the bar with a closed, pronated grip.
- Straighten the arms, but do not lock out the elbows.
- Stand upright with the knees slightly bent and the feet directly under the shoulders (figure 5.5*a*).

Figure 5.5   Standing lat pull-down: *(a)* starting position.

(continued)

Procedure

- Keeping the arms straight, flex the arms at the shoulders, pulling the bar down to the thighs (figure 5.5*b*).
- Slowly extend the shoulders, controlling the bar back to the starting position.
- Throughout the exercise keep the chest up, the hips stationary, and the low back in a neutral position.

Figure 5.5 *(continued)* Standing lat pull-down: *(b)* pull bar down to thighs.

Cable Row

Purpose

To develop upper-back strength with a focus on scapular adductors

Equipment

Cable column, straight bar attachment at waist height

Starting Position

- This drill can be performed standing or sitting in a cable machine.
- In either situation, the shoulders should remain over the hips, and the spine should be in a neutral position (figure 5.6*a*).
- The grip can be pronated, neutral, or supinated; the elbows should be straight; and the scapulae should be relaxed.

Procedure

- Pull the bar into the chest by flexing the elbows and adducting the scapulae (figure 5.6*b*).
- At the end of the range of motion, squeeze the scapulae together and then return to the starting position.
- Throughout the exercise, avoid quick, jerky pulls to reduce the momentum created by the arms and to maximize scapular adductor involvement.

Figure 5.6   Cable row: *(a)* starting position; *(b)* pull the bar to the chest.

Single-Arm Strap Row

Purpose

To develop unilateral upper-body strength in rowing (scapular abduction) with an emphasis on the rhomboids, mid trapezius, rear deltoids, and biceps

Equipment

Cable column, handle attachment

Setup

Hang a strap or ring from a hook on a wall or a pull-up bar.

Starting Position

- Place both feet against a wall, feet just wider than shoulder width.
- Hold the handle or ring in the right hand with the right arm straight and right shoulder relaxed (figure 5.7*a*).
- The left shoulder is rotated left and posterior.

Figure 5.7   Single-arm strap row: *(a)* starting position.

(continued)

- The left hand is held tight into the left chest, the left arm is abducted and perpendicular to the torso, and the elbow is fully flexed.

Procedure

- Row the right hand into the right armpit and reach the left hand as far up the strap as possible (figure 5.7b).
- Lower yourself under control back to the starting position.
- Maintain a straight line from the heels to the shoulders throughout the exercise.

Figure 5.7 *(continued)* Single-arm strap row: *(b)* row the right hand into the armpit and reach the left hand up the strap.

Bent Row

Purpose

To develop upper-body strength in rowing (scapular abduction) with an emphasis on the rhomboids, mid trapezius, rear deltoids, and biceps

Equipment

Barbell, weight plates

Starting Position

- Grip the bar with a closed, pronated grip, keep elbows straight, and rest the bar on the thighs.
- Feet are hip-width apart.
- Flex the hips and knees into a quarter squat.
- Keeping the back neutral, bend forward at the hips until the bar is just above the kneecaps.

Procedure

- Row the bar just below the chest and into the ribs by extending at the shoulders, flexing the elbows, and retracting the shoulder blades.
- Lower the bar under control back to the starting position.

▶ Supine Row

Purpose

To develop upper-body strength in rowing (scapular abduction) with an emphasis on the rhomboids, mid trapezius, rear deltoids, and biceps

Equipment

Bar in a squat rack or dip bars

Setup

- Adjust the catch bars on a squat rack so they are farther than an arm's length from the floor.
- Place a barbell on the catch bars.

Starting Position

- Lie supine with the shoulders slightly posterior to the barbell.
- Grip the bar using a supine or pronated grip.
- Elevate the hips so the body forms a straight line from the heels to the shoulders.

Procedure

- Pull the chest to the bar by flexing the elbows, extending at the shoulders, and retracting the scapulae, pulling them toward the spine.
- Lower yourself back to the starting position.
- Throughout the exercise, keep the body rigid and in a straight line from the heels to the shoulders.

Note

Elevating the feet on a box or ball increases the difficulty of the exercise.

Push-Up

Purpose

To develop upper-body and core strength with an emphasis on the chest, anterior deltoids, and triceps

Starting Position

- Lie prone with the feet and hands on the floor.
- The hands should be placed slightly wider than shoulder-width apart (figure 5.8a).

Procedure

- Flex the elbows, lowering the chest toward the floor (figure 5.8b).
- Stop just before the nose or chest touches the floor and return to the starting position.
- Throughout the exercise, maintain a neutral posture; do not allow the hips to dip toward the floor.

Figure 5.8 Push-up: (a) starting position; (b) lower the chest toward the floor.

Variations

- If you are unable to do push-ups, you can perform bench or band push-ups. Placing the hands on a bench with the feet on the floor or using a loop band hanging from a bar inside a squat rack enables you to perform push-ups while lifting a lower percentage of your body weight. These push-ups can be made more difficult by putting the hands on a 6- or 12-inch (15 or 30 cm) box instead of the bench or by using lighter bands. The goal is to progressively increase the intensity of the push-up until you can perform a regular body-weight push-up.
- If you can easily perform push-ups, you can increase the intensity by either elevating your feet on a box or bench or decreasing stability by placing the hands on a stability ball. Increasing foot height forces you to lift a higher percentage of your body weight and increases the need for core stability. Taking stability away by placing the hands on a stability ball instead of the floor increases the demands on both core strength and shoulder stability.

Single-Arm Cable Push With Twist

Purpose

To develop standing integrated core and upper-body strength in a forward pressing motion. The primary emphasis is on initiating the movement with the hip to develop momentum for the pressing motion.

Equipment

Cable machine with the handle attachment located between the hip and shoulder

Starting Position

- Stand 3 to 4 feet (1 to 1.2 m) from and facing away from the cable machine in a split stance with the right foot forward and the left foot back.
- The handle to the cable machine is in the left hand with the left elbow at shoulder height. The forearm is parallel to the floor, and the elbow is flexed so the hand is directly in front of the right pectoralis major muscle.
- Flex the right upper arm until it is parallel to the floor, the elbow is extended, and the fingers are pointed forward (figure 5.9a).

Procedure

- Initiate the movement by rotating the left hip to the right. (This is a small movement because of the split stance.)
- With the left hand, press the cable forward until the elbow is extended while pulling the right elbow back (figure 5.9b).
- Return to the starting position.

Figure 5.9 Single-arm cable push with twist: (a) starting position; (b) press the cable forward.

SUMMARY

Developing a strength base is crucial in the overall development of the volleyball athlete. The focus of strength training should be on enhancing force production through high-intensity exercises and providing adequate rest to promote recovery. Exercises should be performed in multiple planes of movement and in both bilateral and unilateral stances.

Chapter 6

Power

Simply put, power is the ability to generate force quickly and explosively. People with higher power outputs exhibit higher vertical jumps and increased abilities to accelerate and move quickly. Variations in load, speed of movement, and range of motion are critical in maximizing power development. This is accomplished by implementing load-based power training and plyometric exercises.

Because of the high levels of neural involvement in power training, all-out effort and a high rest-to-work ratio are needed to elicit a positive training response. In both load-based and plyometric training exercises, the speed and distance achieved with a bar, implement, or one's own body weight are the most important factors when determining the load. Force plates and Tendo units can be very helpful in assessing power output and speed. Using these devices, standards of force and speed can be set for each exercise. These standards must be reached before increasing the load of the exercise. A base of strength must be obtained so the athlete can produce adequate levels of force and maximize power output. This chapter addresses load-based power training and plyometrics and presents exercises to improve power output.

LOAD-BASED POWER TRAINING

Load-based power training involves explosively moving a weight or resistance throughout a range of motion. Exercises in this category include Olympic lifts, Olympic lift variations, pause squats, and resisted jumps.

Technique and speed of movement should be the primary focus when performing Olympic lifts. The execution of proper technique and the speed of the bar are the factors that determine whether and when the athlete progresses in weight.

Resisted jumps are beneficial because the movement of jumping can be loaded. We use the VertiMax training system so we can load the athlete through the hips without having a bar on the back, which loads the spine. The resistance is determined by the variable of power emphasized and is categorized as strength-power, power, and speed-power training. When resistance is increased in strength-power training, emphasis is placed more on force development than on velocity. In many cases, a pause is implemented to negate the preload of the muscle at the transition between the eccentric and concentric movement. This pause dissipates the elastic energy and reduces the muscle stretch reflex causing the muscle to do more work. Pure power training focuses more equally on force and velocity with moderate to moderate/light loads that allow for higher movement speed. The preload prior to jumping is reintroduced to take advantage of elastic properties of the muscle tissue and the stretch reflex. Speed-power training uses light loads to obtain high velocities. Variables such as preloading with countermovements, continuous jumps, and range of motion are manipulated to maximize velocity.

Load-based training allows the athlete to perform explosive triple-extension movements of the hip, knee, and ankle through various loading parameters. Sets are performed at low repetition ranges, between two and five, with an emphasis on speed of movement and a high rest-to-work ratio to maximize power output.

▶ Hang Snatch

Purpose

To develop total-body explosive power

Equipment

Olympic barbell, bumper plates, clips

Grip Width Measurement

- Stand tall with one arm abducted out to the side, elbow straight, and hand in a fist.
- Measure the distance from the opposite shoulder to the knuckles of the hand forming a fist.
- This measurement is the starting point for the grip width on the bar.

Starting Position

- Walk the shins up to the barbell.
- Grasp the bar with a closed, pronated grip, hands at the width determined by the grip width measurement protocol.

- Flex at the hips and knees, dropping the butt to the floor and elevating the chest so it faces forward.
- Retract the shoulder blades and rotate the elbows back, activating the rear deltoids.
- Stand tall with the bar in the hands, elbows straight.

Procedure

- Slightly flex the hips and knees.
- Inhale and hold your breath.
- Keep the back in neutral and flex forward through the hips. Keep the bar in contact with the legs and the hands directly under the shoulders.
- Flex forward through the hip until you reach the end range of motion or the bar reaches the top of the knees.
- Keeping the bar tight to the body, drive the hips forward and extend at the hips, knees, and ankles (triple extension).
- At full triple extension, shrug the shoulders to the ears and pull with the arms, keeping the elbows high and the bar tight to the body.
- Drop under the bar, extend the elbows, and retract the scapulae, catching the bar overhead.

Note

Never use lifting straps when performing a snatch. If the weight becomes too heavy to hold, grip the bar with a hook grip. First wrap the thumb around the bar; then grip both the bar and the thumb with the index and middle fingers.

Power Snatch

Purpose

To develop total-body explosive power

Equipment

Olympic barbell, bumper plates, clips

Grip Width Measurement

- Stand tall with one arm abducted out to the side, elbow straight, and hand in a fist.
- Measure the distance from the opposite shoulder to the knuckles of the hand forming a fist.
- This measurement is the starting point for the grip width on the bar.

Starting Position

- Place the barbell on the floor with Olympic weights on each end.
- Walk up to the bar until the shins are against it, feet hip-width apart.
- Grasp the bar with a closed, pronated grip, hands at the width determined by the grip width measurement protocol.
- Sit the hips down so the knees are just above the arches of the feet.
- The back is neutral with the torso flexed slightly forward and the shoulders right above the hands.
- Keep the elbows locked out and retract the shoulder blades to create tension through the arms and take the slack out from between the bar and the weights.

Procedure

- Inhale and hold your breath.
- Keeping the same torso angle and the elbows locked, extend the hips and knees at a moderate to fast pace.
- Once the bar clears the knees, maximally accelerate the bar by driving the hips forward toward the bar, extending at the hips, knees, and ankles (triple extension).
- At full triple extension, shrug the shoulders to the ears and pull with the arms, keeping the elbows high.
- At maximal height of the elbows, flex the hips and knees to drop under the bar. Extend the elbows and retract the scapulae, catching the bar overhead.

Notes

- To perform a proper power snatch, you must get into a solid starting position by creating tension throughout the body and taking the slack out from between the bar and the weights.
- Never use lifting straps when performing a snatch. If the weight becomes too heavy to hold, grip the bar with a hook grip. First wrap the thumb around the bar; then grip both the bar and the thumb with the index and middle fingers.

Jump Shrug From Floor

Purpose

To develop lower-body explosive power

Equipment

Olympic barbell, bumper plates, clips

Starting Position

- Place the barbell on the floor with Olympic weights on each end.
- Walk to the bar until the shins are against it.
- Grasp the bar with a closed, pronated grip, hands shoulder-width apart.
- Sit the hips down so the knees are just above the arches of the feet.
- The back is neutral with the torso flexed slightly forward and the shoulders right above the hands.
- Keep the elbows locked out and retract the shoulder blades to create tension through the arms and take the slack out from between the bar and the weights.

Procedure

- Inhale and hold your breath.
- Keeping the same torso angle and the elbows locked, extend the hips and knees at a moderate to fast pace (figure 6.1a).
- Once the bar clears the knees, drive the hips forward and into a jump (figure 6.1b), extending at the hips, knees, and ankles (triple extension).
- Once the shoulders reach maximal height, release the bar and drop it to the platform (figure 6.1c).

Figure 6.1 Jump shrug from floor: (a) extend hips and knees; (b) drive hips forward into a jump; (c) when the shoulders are at maximal height, release the bar.

Push Jerk

Purpose

To develop total-body explosive power

Equipment

Barbell, squat rack, clips

Starting Position

- Grasp the bar with a closed, pronated grip, hands slightly wider than shoulder width.
- Step under the bar, resting it on the anterior deltoids.
- Flex the upper arms so they are slightly below parallel to the floor.
- Shrug the shoulders to elevate the bar off the collarbones.
- Unrack the bar and stand tall with the chest up and the feet shoulder-width apart.

Procedure

- Inhale and hold your breath during the downward movement.
- Quickly flex the hip and knees, dropping the butt 3 to 4 inches (8 to 10 cm) (figure 6.2a).
- Quickly extend the hips, knees, and ankles.
- The momentum created by the lower body will pop the bar off the shoulders and up (figure 6.2b).

Figure 6.2 Push jerk: (a) downward movement; (b) upward movement, which causes bar to pop off shoulders.

- Finish the excise by pressing the arms above the head while flexing the hips and knees, dropping into a quarter squat under the bar (figure 6.2c).
- Catch the bar with the hands directly over the shoulders.

Figure 6.2 *(continued)* Push jerk: *(c)* press arms overhead and drop into quarter squat.

VERTIMAX

The VertiMax is a piece of equipment used to increase explosive vertical jump. It is unique because it loads the athlete through the hips instead of the spine through the use of a belt pulley and bungee system.

▶ VertiMax Pause, Jump, Squat

Purpose

To develop lower-body strength and power

Equipment

VertiMax

Starting Position

- Place the belt that comes with the VertiMax around the waist with the attachment hooks on the sides of each hip and pointed down.
- Set the desired resistance using the bungee cords on the front or back of the VertiMax platform.
- Step onto the center of the VertiMax platform and attach the bungee cords to the attachment hooks on the belt.
- The feet should be parallel and just outside shoulder width.
- Raise the arms and place the tips of the fingers on the sides of the head.

Procedure

- Sink into a squat by flexing the hips and the knees, keeping the torso as vertical as possible.
- Pause at the end range of motion or when the thighs are parallel to the floor.
- A coach or partner will call out "1-2-up."
- On "up," rapidly extend the hips, knees, and ankles and jump as high as possible.
- After landing, sink into the bottom of the next squat and repeat.

▶ VertiMax Jump Squat Singles

Purpose

To develop lower-body explosive power

Equipment

VertiMax

Starting Position

- Place the belt that comes with the VertiMax around the waist with the attachment hooks on the sides of each hip and pointed down.
- Set the desired resistance using the bungee cords on the front or back of the VertiMax platform.
- Step onto the center of the VertiMax platform and attach bungee cords to the attachment hooks on the belt.
- The feet should be parallel and just outside shoulder width.
- Stand tall and raise the arms and hands overhead.

Procedure

- At a controlled but fast pace, sink into a squat by flexing the hips and the knees and swinging the arms and hands down and back, while keeping the torso as vertical as possible.
- When the thighs are parallel to the floor or you reach your end range of motion, rapidly extend the hips, knees, and ankles and jump as high as possible, simultaneously swinging the hands forward and overhead.
- Land with soft hips and knees. Stand tall and repeat.

Variation: VertiMax Continuous

Performing the VertiMax jump squat continuously develops lower-body speed and power. The execution is the same as the VertiMax jump squat singles, except the repetitions are performed one after another without stopping or pausing.

Integrated Single-Arm Cable Push

Purpose

To develop total-body power by transferring energy from the floor into a pressing movement

Equipment

Cable machine with the handle attachment positioned between the hip and the shoulder

Starting Position

- Stand perpendicular to and 3 to 4 feet (1 to 1.2 m) from the cable machine in a parallel stance.

- With the left side facing the machine, hold the handle of the cable in the left hand with the left elbow at shoulder height, elbow maximally flexed and hand tight to the left pec.

- Flex the right upper arm until it is parallel to the floor, the elbow is extended, and the fingers are pointed forward (figure 6.3a).

Procedure

- Initiate the movement from the floor up by pivoting to the right and extending the left ankle, knee, and hip, creating a slight lag between the left hip and the left shoulder.

- Extend the left elbow, punching the left hand forward while the right elbow flexes and drives back toward the cable column (figure 6.3b).

- Return to the starting position and repeat.

- Repeat on the right side.

Figure 6.3 Integrated single-arm cable push: (a) starting position; (b) pivot to the right and punch.

PLYOMETRICS

Plyometric training is critical because it bridges the gap between the weight room and court performance. It focuses on the velocity component in power development by training the elastic properties of muscle and the neuromuscular system to maximize the stretch response within a muscle. Muscles lengthen (load) in the opposite direction before force is applied in the desired direction. This lengthening creates elastic energy as a result of the resiliency of the tissue, which can be harnessed and used in movement. During the rapid lengthening of a muscle, proprioceptors called muscle spindles activate to send a reflex stimulus to perform a powerful concentric contraction. This neuromuscular reflex can be trained to increase the ability of muscles to contract quicker and perform more powerful muscular contractions.

Plyometric exercises are usually performed with the athlete's body weight, a very light load such as a weight vest, resistance bands, or an implement such as a medicine ball. Basic lower-body plyometric exercises such as hopping, bounding, and jumping are exaggerated versions of fundamental movements performed on the court. Hopping is similar to quick change-of-foot positions, and lateral hopping uses ankle movements similar to those used when shuffling. Bounding is an exaggerated form of accelerating and changing direction. Acceleration and bounding movements are created by a triple extension of the hips, knees, and ankles, producing force into the floor with the foot in the direction opposite the desired direction. Landing and sticking or repeating a bound stresses the body similar to the eccentric loading, while decelerating and cutting. Jump-based plyometrics, such as medicine ball squat push toss and medicine ball back toss, contain the vital component of the triple extension but focus on accelerating force production vertically to improve vertical jump. All-out effort, speed of movement, distance, and technique should be emphasized; adding load or resistance does not need to be a goal.

The high-speed multiplane movements that occur in plyometric exercises cause added eccentric loading and strain on the nervous system of the athlete. Therefore, having a strong base of stability and strength is critical to maximize benefits and prevent injury while performing plyometrics. It is also imperative that exercises be properly progressed and volume appropriately assigned based on the athlete's or team's training history, stability, and strength base as well as practice and match volumes.

Medicine Ball Squat Push Toss

Purpose

To develop total-body speed and explosiveness

Equipment

Medicine ball, facility with a high ceiling

Starting Position

- Stand with the feet just outside shoulder width and the toes slightly pointed out.
- Hold a medicine ball in both hands just above chest height and tight into the body with the elbows maximally flexed.

Procedure

- Inhale and hold your breath.
- At a moderate to fast pace, squat by flexing the hips and knees and keeping the torso as upright as possible until the hips start to posteriorly rotate or the tops of the thighs are parallel to the floor (figure 6.4a).
- Do not pause at the bottom; extend the hips, knees, and ankles into a jump.
- Just prior to full triple extension, start pressing the medicine ball overhead and push it as high in the air as possible (figure 6.4b).
- The goal is maximal vertical height of the medicine ball on the toss.
- Reset the starting position and repeat for the prescribed number of repetitions.

Notes

- Never catch the medicine ball after the toss. Let the ball bounce or hit the floor prior to retrieving it. This reduces the chances of breaking or jamming fingers.
- This exercise can be performed in a full squat as described, a half squat, or a quarter squat.

Figure 6.4   Medicine ball squat push toss: (a) squat until thighs are parallel to floor; (b) jump and push medicine ball overhead.

Medicine Ball Back Toss

Purpose

To develop total-body speed and explosiveness

Equipment

Medicine ball, facility with a high ceiling

Starting Position

- Stand with the feet just outside shoulder width and the toes slightly pointed out.
- Hold a medicine ball in both hands overhead with the elbows locked.

Procedure

- Squat by flexing the hips and knees while keeping the elbows straight and lowering the medicine ball between the legs (figure 6.5a).
- Do not pause at the bottom; extend the hips, knees, and ankles into a jump.
- Just prior to triple extension, swing the ball forward and overhead into maximal shoulder flexion, tossing the ball vertically and behind for maximal vertical height (figure 6.5b).
- The goal is vertical height, but to achieve this using triple extension of the hip, knee, and ankle and maximal shoulder flexion, the ball will land 10 to 15 feet (3 to 4.5 m) behind you.

Figure 6.5 Medicine ball back toss: (a) squat and lower medicine ball between legs; (b) jump and swing ball forward and overhead.

Multidirection Squat and Bound

Purpose

To develop bilateral and uni-lateral multiplane lower-body speed and power

Starting Position

Stand tall with hands overhead.

Procedure

In this drill, a bounding sequence is performed in seven directions (figure 6.6). Complete the pre-scribed number of repetitions of each movement before moving to the next plane of move-ment. For each bound, sink

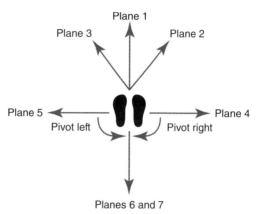

Figure 6.6   The seven directions of the multidirection squat and bound drill.

down into a squat until the hips rotate posteriorly or the upper thighs are parallel to the floor. Maximally extend the hips, knees, and ankles to get maximal distance on the bound. Land on both feet and flex the hips and knees to absorb ground reaction forces. This is the bounding sequence:

- Plane 1: Broad jump (forward)
- Plane 2: Right anterior at 45 degrees
- Plane 3: Left anterior at 45 degrees
- Plane 4: Right lateral
- Plane 5: Left lateral
- Plane 6: Pivot back right
- Plane 7: Pivot back left

Variations

- Stick: Land in the squat position and reset back to the starting posi-tion.
- Counter: Land in the squat position and immediately bound back to the starting position. (For the broad jump, the countermovement is to jump vertically, not back to the starting position.)
- Continuous: Bound out and back to the starting position for the pre-scribed number of repetitions without any pauses. (All continuous broad jumps are performed while moving forward.)

Single-Leg Multidirection Bound

Purpose

To develop unilateral multiplane lower-body balance, speed, power, and deceleration

Starting Position

Stand tall and balance on the left leg.

Procedure

In this drill, a bounding sequence is performed in seven directions, as in the previous drill. (See figure 6.6 for the seven directions.) Complete the prescribed number of repetitions of each movement before moving to the next plane of movement. When performing a bound, sink into a quarter squat. Maximally extend the hip, knee, and ankle to get maximal distance on the bound. Land on the opposite leg and sink into a quarter squat. When landing, do not add any hops or foot manipulations to gain stability. Land cleanly. This is the bounding sequence:

- Plane 1: Broad jump (forward)
- Plane 2: Right anterior at 45 degrees
- Plane 3: Left anterior at 45 degrees
- Plane 4: Right lateral
- Plane 5: Left lateral
- Plane 6: Pivot back right
- Plane 7: Pivot back left

Variations

- Stick: Land in a quarter squat position and hold for 1 1/2 to 2 seconds. Reset back to the starting position.
- Counter: Land in a quarter squat position and immediately bound back to the starting position, holding the landing for 1 1/2 to 2 seconds. Reset back to the starting position.
- Continuous: Bound out and back to the starting position for the prescribed number of repetitions.

Forward Bounding Lunge

Purpose

To develop lower-body speed and explosiveness

Starting Position

- Take a long step forward with the left leg.
- Flex the left hip and knee and right knee so both legs create a 90-degree angle with the upper and lower leg.
- The left knee should be directly over the heel of the left foot, and the right knee should be just off the floor.
- The torso should be vertical with the shoulders directly over the hips.
- Flex the left shoulder until the upper arm is parallel to the floor, and flex the left elbow to 90 degrees.
- Extend the right shoulder and flex the elbow to 90 degrees (figure 6.7a).

Procedure

- Forcefully and rapidly extend the left hip, knee, and ankle while flexing the right hip and driving the right knee forward.
- Simultaneously drive the right elbow down and the left elbow forward, propelling the body maximally forward into the air (figure 6.7b).
- Land in a lunge position with the right leg forward, left leg back, shoulders over hips, left arm flexed, and right arm extended (figure 6.7c).
- Reset and repeat.
- The goal is to achieve maximal distance forward on each bound.

Figure 6.7 Forward bounding lunge: *(a)* starting position with left leg forward; *(b)* propel body forward in the air; *(c)* land in lunge with right leg forward.

▶ Lateral Hop, Hop, Bound

Purpose

To develop lateral foot quickness, explosiveness, and the ability to decelerate

Setup

Tape four parallel lines on the floor. The first and fourth lines are 10 to 12 feet (3 to 3.7 m) apart. The first and second lines and third and fourth lines are 2 feet (60 cm) apart.

Starting Position

Stand to the left of the first line with the shoulders perpendicular to the line. Balance on the left leg.

Procedure

- Hop laterally over the first line.
- Hop laterally over the second line, landing between the second and third lines.
- Bound laterally over the third and fourth lines, sticking the landing in a half squat position on the right foot.
- The hops should be very quick. Focus on building lateral speed and momentum.
- The bound should be explosive. Focus on extending through the hip, knee, and ankle to get distance laterally.
- Stick the landing without additional hops or foot manipulation to gain balance.

Variations

- Stick: Perform a hop, hop, and bound to the opposite foot. Stick the landing for 2 seconds with the hip and knee flexed.
- Counter: Same as the stick with the addition of a bound back to the left. Stick the landing at the starting position for 2 seconds with the hip and knee flexed.
- Continuous: Perform a hop, hop, and bound there and back for multiple repetitions without pausing or sticking the landing until the very last bound (the finish of the drill).

⏵ Forward Hop, Hop, Bound

Purpose

To develop foot quickness, explosiveness, and the ability to decelerate in the sagittal plane. In the second variation, explosiveness and deceleration are also trained in the transverse plane.

Setup

Tape four parallel lines on the floor. The first and fourth lines are 10 to 12 feet (3 to 3.7 m) apart. The first and second lines and third and fourth lines are 2 feet (60 cm) apart.

Starting Position

Stand in front of the first line with shoulders parallel to it. Balance on the left leg.

Procedure

- Hop forward over the first line.
- Hop forward over the second line, landing between the second and third lines.
- Forward bound over the third and fourth lines, sticking the landing in a half squat position on the right foot.
- The hops should be very quick. Focus on building speed and forward momentum.
- The bound should be explosive. Focus on extending through the hip, knee, and ankle, building forward distance.
- Stick the landing without additional hops or foot manipulation to gain balance.

Variations

- Stick: Perform a hop, hop, and bound to the opposite foot. Stick the landing and hold for 2 seconds with the hip and knee flexed.
- Counter: Same as the stick with the addition of a pivot bound to the left Stick for 2 seconds with the hip and knee flexed.
- Continuous: Perform a hop, hop, and bound there and back for multiple repetitions without pausing or sticking the landing until the very last bound (the finish of the drill).

Forward Hop, Hop, Lateral Bound

Purpose

To develop multiplane foot quickness, explosiveness, and the ability to decelerate

Setup

Tape four parallel lines on the floor. The first and fourth lines are 4 1/2 to 5 feet (137 to 152 cm) apart. The first and second lines are 1 1/2 feet (46 cm) apart. The third and fourth lines are 2 feet (60 cm) apart.

Starting Position

Stand in front of the first line with shoulders parallel to the first line. Balance on the left leg.

Procedure

- Hop forward over the first and second lines.
- Hop forward over the third and fourth lines.
- Bound laterally quickly and for maximal distance.
- The hops should be very quick. Focus on building speed and forward momentum.
- The bound should be explosive. Focus on extending through the hip, knee, and ankle, maximizing distance laterally.
- Stick the landing without additional hops or foot manipulation to gain balance.

Variations

- Stick: From the bound, land in a quarter squat position and hold for 1 1/2 to 2 seconds.
- Counter: After landing from the bound, sink into a quarter squat and immediately bound back in the opposite direction.

▶ Back Hop, Hop, Lateral Bound

Purpose

To develop multiplane foot quickness, explosiveness, and the ability to decelerate

Setup

Tape four parallel lines on the floor. The first and fourth lines are 4 to 5 feet (122 to 152 cm) apart. The first and second lines are 1 1/2 feet (46 cm) apart. The third and fourth lines are 2 feet (60 cm) apart.

Starting Position

Stand in front of and facing away from the first line with shoulders parallel to the first line. Balance on the left leg.

Procedure

- Hop backward over the first and second lines.
- Hop backward over the third and fourth lines.
- Bound laterally quickly and for maximal distance.
- The hops should be very quick. Focus on building speed and momentum backward.
- The bound should be explosive. Focus on extending through the hip, knee, and ankle, maximizing distance laterally.
- Stick the landing without additional hops or foot manipulation to gain balance.

Variations

- Stick: From the bound, land in a quarter squat position and hold for 1 1/2 to 2 seconds.
- Counter: After landing from the bound, sink into a quarter squat and immediately bound back in the opposite direction.

Box Hop, Hop, Lateral Bound

Purpose

To develop multiplane foot quickness, explosiveness, and the ability to decelerate

Setup

Tape two sets of four parallel lines each on the floor. The first and fourth lines are 5 to 6 feet (122 to 152 cm) apart. The first and second lines are 1 1/2 feet (46 cm) apart. The third and fourth lines are 2 feet (60 cm) apart. The two sets of lines are 3 to 4 1/2 feet (91 to 137 cm) apart (figure 6.8).

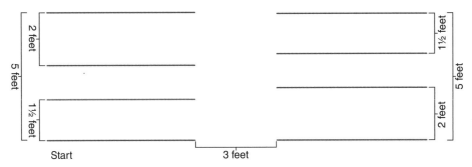

Figure 6.8 Box hop, hop, lateral bound.

Starting Position

Stand in front of the first line with shoulders parallel to the first line. Balance on the left leg.

Procedure

- Hop forward over the first and second lines.
- Hop forward over the third and fourth lines.
- Bound laterally toward and in front of the second set of lines.
- Hop backward over the first and second lines.
- Hop backward over the third and fourth lines.
- Bound laterally to the start of the drill.
- Repeat for the prescribed number of repetitions.
- The hops should be very quick. Focus on building speed and momentum forward and backward.
- The bound should be explosive. Focus on extending through the hip, knee, and ankle, maximizing distance laterally.
- Stick the landing without additional hops or foot manipulation to gain balance.

Box Split Jump

Purpose

To develop unilateral vertical speed and explosiveness

Equipment

12- to 18-inch (30 to 46 cm) plyometric box

Starting Position

- Stand directly in front of the plyometric box.
- Place the left foot on the box, creating an approximate 90-degree angle between the upper and lower leg.
- Flex the shoulder and elbow of the right arm so the upper arm is parallel to the floor and the elbow creates a 90-degree angle.
- Extend the shoulder of the left arm (figure 6.9a).

Procedure

- Extend the left hip, knee, and ankle while flexing the right hip and knee, going into a maximal jump (figure 6.9b).
- At the same time, drive the right elbow down and rapidly bring the left elbow up.
- Land on the box with the left foot followed immediately by the right foot (figure 6.9c).
- Step down (figure 6.9d) and repeat for the prescribed number of repetitions.
- Repeat on the opposite leg.

Figure 6.9 Box split jump: (a) starting position; (b) maximal jump; (c) land on the box; (d) step down.

Line Hops Series

Purpose

To develop foot quickness

Equipment

Court line or 2-inch-wide (5 cm) tape

Procedure

Perform the following hops as quickly as possible for 8 to 10 seconds:

- Lateral hops: Hop side to side over a line.
- Forward and back hops: Hop forward and back over a line.
- Rotate (two feet only): Face the line with one foot over the line and one foot behind the line, toes pointed forward, and feet shoulder-width apart. Rotate the hips back and forth to move the feet over the line in opposite directions.

Variations

- Two feet
- One foot

Single-Leg Ladder Hop Series

Purpose

To develop foot quickness

Equipment

Agility ladder

Procedure

For each drill, repeat with the opposite leg after each run down the ladder.

- Forward: Hop forward in each square down the ladder.
- Backward: Hop backward in each square down the ladder.
- Lateral: Hop laterally in each square down the ladder.
- Slalom: Using one side of the ladder only, hop forward and in and out of the ladder.

Notes

- Focus on performing quick hops with as little floor contact time as possible.
- Land on the forefoot with very little to no heel contact.

Half Wheel Hop

Purpose

To develop multiplane unilateral stability, deceleration, and foot quickness

Setup

Tape six dots, a starting dot in the center and five dots 28 inches (70 cm) away from the center dot in five directions: front, forward angle, lateral, back angle, and back (figure 6.10).

Starting Position

Balance on the left leg on the starting dot.

Procedure

- Pause: Hop to each dot and back to the starting position. At each dot, stick the landing in a quarter squat for 2 seconds, keeping the knee aligned with the hip and foot and the foot flat on the floor. Extend through the hip, knee, and ankle on the hop. Perform the prescribed number of repetitions and switch legs.

- Continuous: Hop to each dot and back to the starting position. Perform hops as quickly as possible with floor contact at the forefoot and the heel remaining off the floor. Finish the drill by sticking the very last hop back to the starting position. Perform the prescribed number of repetitions and switch legs.

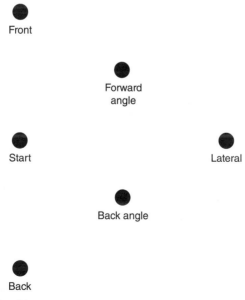

Figure 6.10   Half wheel hop.

Five-Dot Hop

Purpose

To develop multiplane unilateral foot quickness, stability, and deceleration

Setup

Tape five dots in an X formation, measuring 2 1/2 by 4 feet (76 to 122 cm).

Starting Position

Balance on the left leg in the lower left corner of the X dot formation.

Procedure

- Hop from the lower left corner dot to the center dot.
- Hop to the upper left corner dot; then hop to the upper right corner dot.
- Hop back to the center dot; then hop to the lower right dot.
- Finally, hop back to the starting position at the lower left corner dot.
- Perform the circuit twice, sticking the landing in a quarter squat, keeping the knee aligned with the hip and foot and the foot flat on the floor, and holding for 2 seconds.
- Stay on the same foot and perform the circuit twice more as quickly as possible, staying on the forefoot and having as little floor contact time as possible. Repeat on the opposite leg.

Hurdle Hop

Purpose

To develop lower-body explosiveness

Equipment

Five hurdles 6 to 24 inches (15 to 60 cm) high, depending on ability

Starting Position

Stand in front of and facing the hurdles.

Procedure

- One at a time and without pausing, hop over the hurdles.
- Keep the knee in line with the ankle and the foot.
- Focus on quick hops with as little floor contact time as possible.

Variations

- Two legs
- One leg

Depth Jump

Purpose

To develop lower-body explosiveness.

Equipment

Two boxes (height depends on ability)

Setup

Place two boxes 2 to 3 feet (60 to 90 cm) apart.

Starting Position

Stand upright on the first box in a hip-width stance (figure 6.11a).

Procedure

- Drop off the first box (figure 6.11b).
- At floor contact, immediately jump onto the second box (figure 6.11c).
- Keep the knees aligned with the hips and ankles.
- Focus on having as little floor contact time as possible.

Figure 6.11 Depth jump: (a) starting position; (b) drop off first box; (c) immediately jump onto second box..

Note

The ability to minimize floor contact time dictates the height of both boxes.

Variations

- Two legs
- One leg

Knee Tuck Jump

Purpose

To develop lower-body explosiveness

Starting Position

Stand upright with the feet hip-width apart.

Procedure

- Jump in the air for maximal height.
- Raise the knees to the chest (figure 6.12).
- When landing, drive the forefoot into the floor to quickly accelerate into the next jump.
- Repeat for the prescribed number of repetitions.
- Throughout the exercise, keep the knees in line with the hips and ankles.
- Focus on having as little floor contact time as possible.

Figure 6.12   Knee tuck jump.

Box Plyometric Push-Up

Purpose

To develop upper-body explosiveness in a pressing motion and eccentrically lengthen the pecs

Equipment

Two boxes 2 to 12 inches (5 to 30 cm) high, depending on ability

Setup

Place two boxes on the floor about 3 feet (1 m) apart.

Starting Position

Start in a push-up position with a hand on each box and the feet on the floor (figure 6.13a).

Procedure

- Drop the hands medially off the boxes and onto the floor.
- Immediately flex the elbows and sink into a push-up when the hands hit the floor (figure 6.13b).
- Lower into the push-up until the elbows are at least at 90-degree angles or the chest is just above the floor.
- Without pausing at the bottom, change direction and create momentum by extending at the elbows and wrists. Push through the hands and propel them off the floor (figure 6.13c).
- In the air, move the hands back onto the boxes and sink into another push-up (figure 6.13d).

Figure 6.13 Box plyometric push-up: (a) starting position with hands on boxes; (b) drop hands off boxes and sink into push-up with hands on floor; (c) extend at elbows and wrists to push hands off floor; (d) return hands to boxes and do another push-up.

Note

It is important to maintain a neutral spine throughout the exercise. Do not allow the hips or low back to dip toward the floor.

Variations

This exercise can be performed doing single or continuous repetitions.

SUMMARY

Power training, both load-based and plyometrics, is critical to maximize an athlete's ability to jump high and accelerate and change direction quickly. When performing exercises for power, athletes must give 100 percent effort to move the weight, the implement, or themselves as fast and as far as possible during every repetition. The stimulus while performing the maximal effort is what triggers the nervous system to adapt and perform quicker, more explosive muscle contractions.

Chapter 7

Quickness and Agility

Agility training focuses on the ability to move quickly, accelerate, decelerate, and change direction efficiently. Agility training in volleyball must also focus on visual reaction time because the majority of quick movements are initiated by visually reacting to a ball. This chapter addresses foot quickness, basic movement technique, and exercise progression and presents exercises to improve agility.

FOOT QUICKNESS

Quickness is defined as the ability to move one's feet quickly in multiple planes of movement. This movement is created mostly at the foot and ankle through the elasticity of tendons and ground reaction forces. This is important because a volleyball player has a split second to react and reposition the body to make decisions and plays. To truly enhance quickness, athletes must combine quickness or foot quickness drills with plyometrics to enhance the rate of force production and the elasticity of the muscles and tendons and to increase neuromuscular efficiency. This is usually attained using hopping drills and box depth jumps.

Agility Ladder

Purpose

To improve foot quickness

Equipment

Agility ladder

Lateral Two Feet In

- Stand at the left end of the ladder with hips perpendicular to the rungs.
- Push into the floor with the left foot and side step into the ladder with the right foot (figure 7.1).
- Step over the first rung of the ladder with the left foot.
- Repeat in a lateral shuffle formation through the length of the ladder, keeping the hips square and parallel to the side of the ladder.
- Repeat at the starting position facing the opposite direction.

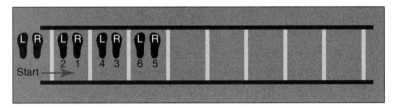

Figure 7.1   Lateral two feet in drill.

Side In and Out

- Stand at the left end of the ladder directly behind the first square, facing and hips parallel to the length of the ladder.
- Step the right foot forward into the first square of the ladder (figure 7.2).
- Step the left foot into the first square of the ladder.
- Step the right foot back and to the right out of the first square and behind the second square of the ladder.
- Step the left foot back and to the right next to the right foot.

- Repeat stepping in and out of the ladder and moving to the right down the ladder.
- Repeat at the starting position on the opposite side of the ladder facing the other direction.

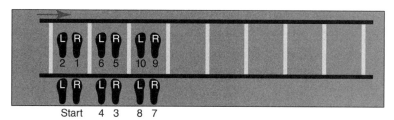

Figure 7.2   Side in and out drill.

Side Rotate Forward (One Foot In)

- Stand at the left end of the ladder behind and to the left of the first square. Face the ladder with the hips parallel to the length of the ladder.
- Perform a crossover step with the left foot in front of the right and into the first square (figure 7.3).
- Take a small step to the right with the right foot.
- Step with the left foot out and just behind the first square of the ladder.
- To assist in the crossover step motion, the hips should rotate.
- Repeat, performing a crossover step with the left foot and a transition step with the right foot, and then stepping back and out of the ladder with the left foot for the length of the ladder.
- Repeat at the starting position on the opposite side of the ladder and perform the crossover step with the right foot.

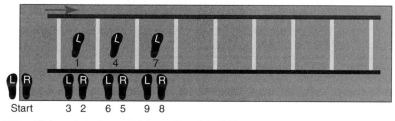

Figure 7.3   Side rotate forward (one foot in) drill.

Side Rotate Back (One Foot In)

- Stand at one end of the ladder facing away with the hips parallel to the length of the ladder. The right foot is positioned farther from the first rung.
- Pivot and step with the left foot back into the first square of the ladder (figure 7.4).
- Make a small transition step to the left with the right foot.
- Step with the left foot out of the ladder and in front of the second square. Align the hips to be parallel with the length of the ladder.
- Repeat, stepping back and pivoting in and out of the ladder with the left foot and taking small transition steps to the left with the right foot for the length of the ladder.
- Repeat at the starting position on the other side of the ladder, facing the other direction.

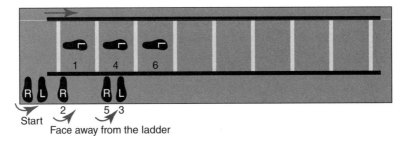

Figure 7.4　Side rotate back (one foot in) drill.

Icky Shuffle (One Foot In and One Foot Out)

- Stand at one end of the ladder, facing and hips parallel to the rungs and the left foot outside and right foot inside the first square.
- Step with the left foot into the first square of the ladder (figure 7.5).
- Step with the right foot to the right and outside the first square of the ladder.
- Step with the left foot forward into the second square of the ladder.
- Step with the right foot into the second square of the ladder.
- Step with the left foot outside and to the left of the second square of the ladder.
- Step with the right foot forward into the third square.
- Repeat through the length of the ladder.

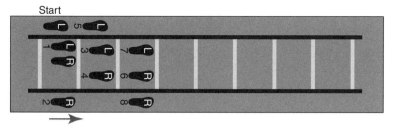

Figure 7.5   Icky shuffle (one foot in and one foot out) drill.

Icky Shuffle (Two Feet Out)

- Stand at one end of the ladder facing and with hips parallel to the rungs and both feet to the left of the first square.
- Step with the right foot to the right into the first square of the ladder (figure 7.6).
- Step with the left foot to the right into the first square of the ladder.
- Step with the right foot to the right out of the first square of the ladder.
- Step with the left foot to the right out of the first square of the ladder.
- Step with the left foot forward and to the left into the second square of the ladder.
- Step the right foot forward and to the left into the second square of the ladder.
- Repeat, stepping both feet in each box and both feet lateral of each box through the length of the ladder.

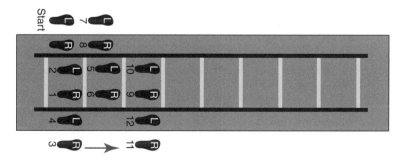

Figure 7.6   Icky shuffle (two feet out) drill.

▶ Lateral Three-Line Agility

Purpose

To improve foot quickness

Setup

Tape three lines parallel to each other on the floor 2 to 3 feet (60 to 76 cm) apart, depending on your height.

Starting Position

Stand with the hips and knees slightly flexed and the feet straddling one of the outside lines.

Procedure

- Step with the outside leg over the line.
- Repeat, alternating steps over each line until the other foot gets outside the third line.
- Change direction quickly and return to the starting position.
- Repeat for a specified amount of time.

Note

Do not hop; take quick steps. One foot should be on the floor at all times.

▶ Forward-and-Back Three-Line Agility

Purpose

To improve foot quickness

Setup

Tape three lines parallel to each other on the floor and 2 to 2 1/2 feet (60 to 76 cm) apart, depending on your height.

Starting Position

Stand with the hips and knees flexed, the shoulders slightly behind the knees, and the toes perpendicular and just behind the first line.

Procedure

- Step one foot over the line and then the other.
- Repeat, alternating steps over each line until both feet get outside the third line.
- Change direction quickly, stepping back over the lines to the starting position.
- Repeat for a specified amount of time.

Note

The torso position should remain unchanged throughout the drill with the shoulders positioned slightly behind the knees.

AGILITY

The ability to react, accelerate, and decelerate quickly and efficiently in multiple planes of movement is critical to the game of volleyball. Volleyball, like other hitting sports, is unique in that movement is caused by a reaction to the ball. Also, most quick defensive movements are made from a stationary position. As a result, acceleration training should have a higher priority than change-of-direction training. This section addresses proper movement mechanics as well as strategies to enhance acceleration and deceleration. When performing quickness and agility drills, athletes need to focus on technique and follow proper exercise progressions.

Proper technique begins with a proper athletic starting position, which we term *go posture.* In this posture, the hips, knees, and ankles are flexed, the shoulders are just behind the knees, the feet are flat on the floor with the body weight shifted toward the forefeet, the back is in a neutral posture, and the eyes are facing the horizon (figure 7.7). When in go posture, the center of gravity is over the feet, and the shin and torso angles are identical.

Figure 7.7   Go posture.

In addition to being in the go posture, volleyball athletes should follow these general rules:

- All movement is created by pushing into the floor with the foot in the direction opposite the desired direction of travel.
- Acceleration is achieved by extending through the hips, knees, and ankles.
- Deceleration is achieved by flexing the hips, knees, and ankles into a squat position.
- All-out effort is needed to create a stimulus large enough to cause the body to adapt, which in turn increases performance.
- Adequate rest time is needed for working at a high capacity and maintain proper mechanics. Work-to-rest ratios should be a minimum of 1:3 and can increase to 1:5. The best way to implement

proper work-to-rest ratios is to build in natural rest periods by using a certain group size (e.g., four athletes per group would result in a work-to-rest ratio of 1:3).

Proper exercise progression is critical to maximize the training effect. The following five-step progression, in which each step prepares the athlete to perform efficient movement at the next step, should be used. The time spent at each step depends on the training age of the athlete and the team. Proper movement mechanics should be the primary emphasis throughout each step.

Step 1: Drills should be performed in a single plane of movement. Focus is on the biomechanics of acceleration and deceleration starting in and returning to go posture. We term these drills *singles* because a specific single distance is achieved or a pause is implemented before a change of direction.

Step 2: Drills are integrated with changes of direction or continuous agility.

Step 3: Drills are performed in multiple planes of movement.

Step 4: Drills are initiated by reacting to a single visual cue from go posture.

Step 5: Drills are initiated by reacting to a visual cue followed by one or more visual cues that initiate a change in direction

It is important to note that maximizing acceleration and deceleration requires stability, strength, and power. Stability, strength, and power training are needed in concert with agility training to optimize your ability to accelerate and decelerate.

Three-Shuffle Drill

Purpose

To learn proper mechanics and improve foot quickness in a shuffle movement

Starting Position

Go posture

Procedure

- On the coach's command of "Go," take three shuffle steps to the right.
- To start the movement, focus on pushing the inside of the left forefoot into the floor to propel the body to the right.

- Pause, reset in go posture if necessary, and repeat to the left on the coach's command.
- Keep the toes pointed forward and the weight on the forefoot throughout the exercise.
- Repeat for the prescribed number of repetitions with pauses between repetitions and the coach initiating each movement with a command.

▶ Backpedal Intervals

Purpose

To learn proper mechanics and improve foot quickness in a backpedal

Starting Position

Begin in go posture on the 10-foot (3 m) line facing the end line.

Procedure

- On the coach's whistle or "go" command, backpedal 10 feet (3 m) to the center line and stop in go posture.
- Initiate the movement by pushing the left forefoot into the floor and propelling the body backward.
- The shoulders should remain slightly behind the kneecaps throughout the drill.
- Movement is created by extending the knees and ankles and driving the forefeet into the floor.
- When decelerating into go posture from a backpedal, the hips, knees, and ankles flex, sinking the butt down and slightly bringing the shoulders forward to counterbalance momentum.
- Repeat for three more 10-foot (3 m) intervals on the coach's command.

Crossover Step

Purpose

To learn proper mechanics and improve lateral sprint acceleration

Starting Position

Go posture

Procedure

- On the coach's command of "Go," perform a single crossover step to the right and then sink back into go posture.
- To start the movement, focus on pushing the inside of the left forefoot into the floor to propel the body to the right (figure 7.8*a*).

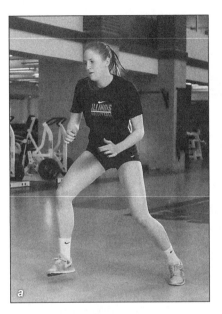

Figure 7.8   Crossover step: *(a)* push off left forefoot to move right and *(b)* bring left knee to the right; *(c)* bring left forefoot down past the right foot and *(d)* square hips and sink back down into go posture.

- As the body moves to the right, the right foot must lift off the floor. Rotate the foot to the right until it points in the direction of travel, and take a small step to the right.
- Drive the left knee across the body to the right by flexing the hip and knee (figure 7.8*b*).
- At the same time, drive the right elbow back and the left elbow across the body to the right to quickly turn the torso in the direction of travel.
- Drive the left forefoot down into the floor just past the right foot (figure 7.8*c*).
- Square the hips back to the starting direction and sink back down by flexing the hips and knees into go posture (figure 7.8*d*).
- Pause and repeat to the left on the coach's command.

Forward Acceleration

Purpose

To learn and improve forward acceleration

Starting Position

Stand in go posture at the court's baseline facing the court.

Procedure

- On the coach's command of "Go," sprint forward 20 feet (6 m) through the near 10-foot (3 m) line.
- Initiate movement by pushing the left forefoot into the floor, creating the momentum to move forward.
- The right foot must lift up and take a small step to move the body forward.
- The left leg then flexes at the hip and knee, creating a 90-degree angle between the thigh and the torso.
- Drive the left forefoot into the floor by extending the hip, knee, and ankle.
- Repeat, alternating flexing the hip, knee, and ankle of one leg and extending the hip, knee, and ankle of the opposite leg in a piston-like fashion.
- The arms should be bent at 90 degrees at the elbows, and movement should be generated by flexion and extension at the shoulder.

Note

Watch out for false steps and correct them. False steps are additional movements which can slow down an athlete's reaction time. They are common when an athlete accelerates forward out of a bilateral stance. Instead of the athlete stepping forward to create momentum to move forward, they first take a step back prior to moving forward. This step back is inefficient, slowing reaction time and the athlete's ability to make a play on the ball.

▶ Pivot Sprint

Purpose

To learn proper mechanics and improve acceleration when turning and running down a ball

Starting Position

Stand in go posture at the 10-foot (3 m) line, facing the center line.

Procedure

- On "Go" or a whistle, turn and sprint 20 feet (6 m) from the 10-foot (3 m) line to the end line.
- Initiate the movement by pushing the inside of the left forefoot into the floor, creating momentum back and to the right.
- The right foot must lift off the floor, open to the right, and take a small step toward the end line to allow momentum to continue in the desired direction.
- The left leg then slightly crosses the midline of the body as the hip, knee, and ankle flex.
- Simultaneously, drive the right elbow back and the left elbow across the body to the left to help the body turn and in the direction of travel.
- Quickly and forcefully drive the left forefoot into the floor by extending the hip, knee, and ankle.
- Repeat, alternating flexing the hip, knee, and ankle of one leg and extending the hip, knee, and ankle of the opposite leg in a piston-like fashion.
- The arms should be bent at 90 degrees at the elbows, and movement should be generated by flexion and extension at the shoulder.
- Repeat, initiating movement with the right foot.

Backpedal and Sprint

Purpose

To improve efficiency while transitioning from a backpedal to a sprint

Starting Position

Stand in go posture at the center line.

Procedure

- Backpedal 10 feet (3 m) from the center line to the 10-foot (3 m) line. Pause in go posture; then sprint forward to the starting position.
- Repeat for the prescribed number of repetitions.
- Initiate the movement by pushing the left forefoot into the floor.
- Throughout the entire drill, the butt should stay down, the shoulders should be right over the knees, and the angle of the back should stay consistent.

▶ Forward Sprint to Pivot Sprint

Purpose

To improve efficiency when decelerating and then accelerating in the opposite direction

Starting Position

Stand in go posture at the end line facing the court.

Procedure

- Sprint forward to and decelerate at the 10-foot (3 m) line.
- Initiate a pivot sprint by pushing the left forefoot into the floor and driving the right elbow back and the left elbow across the body to help turn the hips and torso.
- Sprint through the right corner of the baseline.

Note

To decelerate quickly and efficiently to change directions, flex the hips and knees, drop the butt to the floor, and bring the shoulders forward over the knees.

Lateral Sprint

Purpose

To improve lateral sprint acceleration

Starting Position

Stand in go posture behind and perpendicular to the 10-foot (3 m) line.

Procedure

- Turn and sprint right 20 feet (6 m), decelerating into go posture at the end line.
- Turn and sprint left through the 10-foot (3 m) line.
- To sprint to the right, push off the floor with the inside portion of the left forefoot.
- Drive the right elbow back and the left elbow across the body to turn the hips and torso in the direction of travel.

Two-Shuffle Lateral Sprint

Purpose

To improve efficiency and acceleration while transitioning from a shuffle to a sprint

Starting Position

Stand in go posture behind and perpendicular to the sideline.

Procedure

- Perform two shuffle steps to the right; then turn and sprint through the opposite sideline.
- The transition from shuffle to sprint should be performed with the same technique as described in the crossover step drill.

Multidirection Agility (Short)

Purpose

To improve efficiency in performing multidirection changes of direction

Setup

Tape nine dots per station to the floor: a center dot and eight dots in a circle 6 feet (2 m) from the center.

Starting Position

Begin in go posture, straddling the center dot.

Procedure

- Sprint forward and backpedal to the starting dot.
- Shuffle step to the right at a forward angle and shuffle step back to the starting dot.
- Shuffle step to the right and shuffle step back to the starting dot.
- Shuffle step to the right at a back angle and shuffle step back to the starting dot.
- Backpedal; then sprint back to the starting dot.
- Shuffle step to the left at a back angle and shuffle step back to the starting dot.
- Shuffle step to the left and shuffle back to the starting dot.
- Shuffle step to the left at a forward angle and shuffle step back to the starting dot.

Notes

- Throughout the drill, focus on pushing through the floor with the forefoot to initiate movement in the opposite direction. Keep the body weight over the forefoot, and keep the butt down and shoulders just behind the kneecaps.
- Keep the shoulders square and facing forward throughout the entire drill.

Multidirection Agility (Long)

Purpose

To improve efficiency and acceleration while performing multiple changes of direction

Setup

Tape a dot to the floor, centered between the 10-foot (3 m) line and the end line.

Starting Position

Begin in go posture straddling the dot and facing the 10-foot (3 m) line.

Procedure

- Backpedal to the end line; then sprint to the starting dot.
- Sprint to the left corner of the end line; then sprint to the starting dot.

- Shuffle to the left to the sideline; then shuffle back to the starting dot.
- Sprint to the left corner of the 10-foot (3 m) line; then sprint back to the starting dot.
- Sprint forward to the 10-foot (3 m) line; then turn and sprint though the starting dot.
- Repeat, this time moving right on the angle and lateral sprints.

Note

When changing direction, always turn toward the center of the court.

Backpedal Two Shuffle

Purpose

To improve efficiency while transitioning from a backpedal to a shuffle

Starting Position

Begin in go posture at the center line.

Procedure

- Backpedal to the 10-foot (3 m) line; then perform two shuffle steps to the right.
- Throughout the drill, maintain the same torso to shin angle.
- Repeat the drill, shuffling to the left after the backpedal.

Sprint Two Shuffle

Purpose

To improve efficiency while transitioning from a sprint to a shuffle

Starting Position

Begin in go posture at the baseline, facing the court.

Procedure

- Sprint forward to the 10-foot (3 m) line; then perform two shuffle steps to the right.
- If you make a false step when starting the drill, return to the starting position and begin again.
- Change direction quickly by flexing the hips and knees prior to moving into the shuffle.
- Repeat, shuffling to the left after the sprint.

Pro Agility

Purpose

To improve acceleration and deceleration

Setup

Tape a line on the floor down the center of the court.

Starting Position

Begin in go posture, straddling the taped line on the center of the court.

Procedure

- Sprint to the left to the sideline, touching the left foot to the sideline.
- Turn and sprint to the right to the opposite sideline, touching the right foot to the sideline.
- Turn and sprint through the starting position.

Note

Always turn in the same direction.

Tennis Ball Toss

Purpose

To improve acceleration and eye–hand coordination when reacting to visual cues

Equipment

Five tennis balls

Starting Position

Begin in go posture 15 feet (4.6 m) from and facing the coach.

Procedure

- The coach throws a tennis ball using a bounce pass. React to the coach's throw and catch the tennis ball.
- Once you catch the ball, toss it back to the coach and return to the starting position.
- Once you are set in go posture, the coach throws another ball.

Notes

- The coach should vary the throws, changing speed, direction, and the height of the bounce.

- For the majority of the tosses, the coach should let you reset in go posture to work on acceleration and reaction from a standstill. However, every once in a while, a toss can be included prior to resetting in the center to keep you on your toes.

▶ Single-Plane Mirror Drill

Purpose

To improve the ability to react to a visual stimulus in a single plane of movement and change direction

Starting Position

Two athletes face each other in go posture centered between the 10-foot (3 m) line and the end line.

Procedure

- One athlete is the lead, and the other athlete is the chase.
- The lead athlete dictates the drill by shuffling or sprinting laterally, changing directions at any time.
- The chase athlete mirrors the lead athlete's movements.
- The drill lasts 8 to 10 seconds.

Note

Athletes always face each other when shuffling or turn toward each other when changing direction while sprinting.

▶ Cross Mirror Drill

Purpose

To improve the ability to react to a visual stimulus in multiple planes of movement and change direction

Setup

Tape two sets of five dots in the shape of a cross to the floor in the back 20 feet (6 m) of the court. The cross dimensions are 20 feet (6 m) wide and 15 feet (4.6 m) long.

Starting Position

Two athletes stand in go posture, straddling the center dots of their crosses and facing one another.

Procedure

- One athlete is the lead, and the other athlete is the chase.
- The lead athlete dictates the drill by shuffling, sprinting, or backpedaling within the dimensions of the cross.
- The chase athlete mirrors the lead athlete's movements.
- Each rep is performed for 8-10 seconds.

Rules

- When the lead athlete moves in a direction, she must go all the way to the end of the arm of the cross.
- The lead athlete must return to the center before choosing another direction in which to travel.
- The lead athlete can sprint only to the forward dot and then must backpedal back to the center.
- The lead athlete can backpedal only to the back dot and then must sprint forward.

REACT DRILLS

The react agility drills in this section use lights that are triggered by a handheld remote. Hand gestures showing the athletes where to go can also be used. These drills are volleyball specific in that they are initiated by a visual cue to which athletes must react with a change of direction.

React Three Shuffle

Purpose

To improve shuffle reaction time and acceleration initiated from a visual cue

Setup

Position two reaction lights on boxes that are 5 feet (1.5 m) tall and 8 feet (2.4 m) apart on the center line of a court.

Starting Position

Two athletes perform the drill at the same time, each standing in go posture between the lights on opposite 10-foot (3 m) lines.

Procedure

- The drill is initiated when the one of the lights turns on.
- Perform three shuffle steps in the direction of the light and then three shuffle steps back to the starting position.
- Focus on initiating movement by pushing the foot into the floor in the direction opposite the desired direction of travel; move with quick flicks of the ankle.
- Stay on the forefoot throughout the shuffles, and keep the feet forward.
- Repeat when the next light turns on.

Variations

This drill can be performed with pauses between repetitions, in a continuous fashion, or using a combination of the two.

React Lateral Sprint

Purpose

To improve turn and sprint reaction time and acceleration initiated from a visual cue

Setup

Position two reaction lights on boxes that are 5 feet (1.5 m) tall and 8 feet (2.4 m) apart on the center line of a court.

Starting Position

Two athletes perform the drill at the same time, each standing between the lights on opposite 10-foot (3 m) lines.

Procedure

- The drill is initiated when one of the lights turns on.
- If the left light turns on, turn and sprint through the left sideline.
- If the right light turns on, turn and sprint through the right sideline.
- Focus on crossover step mechanics, initiating movement by pushing the foot into the floor in the direction opposite the desired direction of travel, and using the arms to turn the trunk and hips.

React Forward Sprint

Purpose

To improve forward sprint reaction time and acceleration initiated from a visual cue

Setup

Position three reaction lights on boxes that are 5 feet (1.5 m) tall and staggered 4 feet (1.2 m) apart on the center line of a court.

Starting Position

Stand in go posture just in front of the end line facing the reaction lights.

Procedure

- The drill is initiated when one of the lights turns on.
- Sprint to the light that turns on and decelerate, stopping just in front of it.
- Focus on initiating movement by pushing the foot into the floor in the direction opposite the desired direction of travel.

React Pivot Sprint

Purpose

To improve pivot sprint reaction time and acceleration initiated from a visual cue

Setup

Position three reaction lights on boxes that are 5 feet (1.5 m) tall and staggered 4 feet (1.2 m) apart on the center line of a court.

Starting Position

Two athletes perform the drill at the same time, each standing directly behind the center light on opposite 10-foot (3 m) lines.

Procedure

- The drill is initiated when one of the lights turns on.
- If the left light turns on, turn and sprint to the left corner.
- If the center light turns on, turn and sprint to the baseline directly behind the light.
- If the right light turns on, turn and sprint to the right corner.
- Focus on initiating movement by pushing the foot into the floor in the direction opposite the desired direction of travel and using the arms to turn the trunk and hips.

React Forward Sprint and Lateral Sprint

Purpose

To improve multiplane reaction time and acceleration initiated by two separate visual cues

Setup

Position three reaction lights on boxes that are 5 feet (1.5 m) tall and staggered 4 feet (1.2 m) apart on the center line of a court.

Starting Position

Two athletes perform the drill at the same time, each standing directly behind the center light on opposite baselines.

Procedure

- When the center light turns on, sprint forward.
- Before reaching the center light, you will see either the right or left light turn on. Sprint laterally in that direction through the sideline and out of the court (e.g., if the right light turns on, immediately stop forward progress and turn and sprint out of the court to the right).
- Focus on initiating movement by pushing the foot into the floor in the direction opposite the direction of travel without taking false steps.

React Forward Sprint and Pivot Sprint

Purpose

To improve multiplane reaction time and acceleration initiated by two separate visual cues

Setup

Position three reaction lights on boxes that are 5 feet (1.5 m) tall and staggered 4 feet (1.2 m) apart on the center line of a court.

Starting Position

Two athletes perform the drill at the same time, each standing directly behind the center light on opposite baselines.

Procedure

- When the center light turns on, sprint forward.
- Before reaching the center light, you will see either the right, left, or center light turn on. Immediately stop forward progression and turn and sprint straight back or to a back corner of the court. For example, if the left light is lit, sprint out of the back left corner. If the center light is lit, turn and sprint straight back through the end line.

- Focus on dropping the hips and getting low to decelerate forward motion, and execute proper pivot sprint mechanics to accelerate out of the cut.

React Backpedal and Sprint

Purpose

To improve multiplane reaction time and acceleration initiated by two separate visual cues

Setup

Position three reaction lights on boxes that are 5 feet (1.5 m) tall and staggered 4 feet (1.2 m) apart on the center line of a court.

Starting Position

Two athletes perform the drill at the same time, each standing directly behind the center light just inside opposite 10-foot (3 m) lines.

Procedure

- When the center light turns on, backpedal.
- Before reaching the end line, you will see the right, left, or center light turn on. Sprint forward to the designated light. On the backpedal, focus on initiating movement by pushing the foot into the floor in the direction opposite the desired direction of travel and keeping the hips flexed and shoulders above the knees.
- On the sprint, focus on decelerating quickly by flexing the hips and knees and accelerating out to the light quickly.

React Backpedal and Lateral Sprint

Purpose

To improve multiplane reaction time and acceleration initiated by two separate visual cues

Setup

Position three reaction lights on boxes that are 5 feet (1.5 m) tall and staggered 4 feet (1.2 m) apart on the center line of a court.

Starting Position

Two athletes perform the drill at the same time, each standing directly behind the center light just inside opposite 10-foot (3 m) lines.

Procedure

- When the center light turns on, backpedal.
- Before reaching the end line, you will see the right or left light turn on. Turn and sprint laterally through the sideline in the designated direction. For example, if the left light turns on, immediately stop backward progression and turn and sprint out of the court to the left. On the backpedal, focus on initiating movement by pushing the foot into the floor in the direction opposite the desired direction of travel and keeping the hips flexed and shoulders above the knees.
- On the lateral cut, focus on decelerating rapidly by flexing the hips and knees and accelerating out of the court quickly.

React Backpedal and Three Shuffle

Purpose

To improve multiplane reaction time and acceleration initiated by two separate visual cues

Setup

Position three reaction lights on boxes that are 5 feet (1.5 m) tall and staggered 4 feet (1.2 m) apart on the center line of a court.

Starting Position

Two athletes perform the drill at the same time, each standing directly behind the center light just inside opposite 10-foot (3 m) lines.

Procedure

- When the center light turns on, backpedal.
- Before reaching the end line, you will see the right or left light turn on. Perform three shuffles in that direction. For example, if the left light turns on, immediately stop backward progression and perform three shuffle steps to the left. On the backpedal, focus on initiating movement by pushing the foot into the floor in the direction opposite the direction of travel and keeping the hips flexed and shoulders above the knees.
- On the change of direction, focus on decelerating quickly by flexing the hips and knees and quickly moving into the three shuffle steps.

React Forward Sprint and Two Shuffle

Purpose

To improve multiplane reaction time and acceleration initiated by two separate visual cues

Setup

Position three reaction lights on boxes that are 5 feet (1.5 m) tall and staggered 4 feet (1.2 m) apart on the center line of a court.

Starting Position

Stand in go posture just in front of the end line, facing the reaction lights.

Procedure

- When the center light turns on, sprint forward.
- Before reaching the center light, you will see either the right or left light turn on. Perform three shuffle steps in that direction. For example, if the left light turns on, immediately stop forward progression and perform two shuffle steps to the left. On the sprint, focus on pushing through the floor to initiate movement instead of picking up the foot to move forward.
- On the change of direction, focus on decelerating quickly by flexing the hips and knees and quickly moving into the two shuffle steps.

SUMMARY

Agility is about harnessing all of the components of training—stability, strength, and power—and turning them into efficient movements. Exercises should progress from single plane to multiplane and from verbal starts to more volleyball-specific visual reactive starts. The emphasis should be on basic movement mechanics, effort, and recovery. Do not fall into the trap of turning agility sessions into conditioning sessions. Athletes need time to recover during agility training and should perform conditioning drills separately.

Chapter 8

Core Training and Shoulder Prehab

The core is much more than the abdominals. It encompasses all the structures and muscles of the torso and pelvis. It is the bridge between the upper and lower extremities, transferring energy and creating stability during all functional movement. A strong core, including a mobile and stable thoracic spine, is a key contributor to shoulder health. Shoulder prehab should include developing a base of isolated strength and integrating the core and shoulders to create more functional movement patterns. This chapter addresses the importance of hip activation, ways to train the core for stability and power, and functional shoulder prehab. Exercises are presented to improve these areas.

GLUTE ACTIVATION

The gluteus maximus (or glute) is the posterior bridge between the pelvis and the lower limbs. Its main function is to extend the hip joint. Many athletes have developed poor recruitment patterns by using primarily the hamstrings or the lumbar spine to extend the hip instead of the gluteus maximus. This can cause hamstring strains or increase stress on the facet joints of the lumbar spine. Focus should be on proper hip extension through glute activation while maintaining stability through the lumbar spine. Glute activation progression starts with learning the difference between hip extension and lumbar extension in a single plane, then progresses to loading the hip in multiple planes of movement and finally adding knee flexion to add more hamstring involvement.

Cook Hip Lift

Purpose

To learn to use the gluteus maximus instead of the hamstrings or lumbar spine as the primary hip extensor

Equipment

Tennis ball

Starting Position

- Lie supine on the floor with a tennis ball between the right ASIS (anterior superior iliac spine, or the front hip bone) and the right last rib.
- Flex the right hip and knee, pulling the thigh toward the chest with the hands and compressing the tennis ball into the abdomen.
- Flex the left knee, bringing the heel into the butt.
- Dorsiflex the left ankle so the toe is off the floor and the weight is through the heel.

Procedure

- Extend the left hip by driving through the left heel (figure 8.1).
- Keep pressure on the tennis ball so it doesn't fall off the hip.
- Hold for 5 seconds.
- Repeat on the opposite leg.

Note

Keeping the ball pressed between the thigh and the abdomen forces you to extend through the hip, not the lumbar spine.

Figure 8.1   Cook hip lift.

Bench Hip Extension

Purpose

To develop strength in hip extension with primary emphasis on glute strength

Equipment

Weight bench

Starting Position

- Lie supine on a weight bench with the shoulder blades and upper arms abducted, elbows extended.
- The heels should be directly underneath the knees with the toes pointed forward and the feet flat on the floor.

Procedure

- Lift the right leg by extending the right knee.
- Extend the left hip, squeezing the left glute (figure 8.2).
- Hold for 2 seconds.
- Relax the left hip, let it flex 4 to 5 inches (10 to 12 cm), and then repeat. Repeat on the opposite leg.

Figure 8.2 Bench hip extension.

▶ Supine Lateral Ball Roll

Purpose

To develop multiplane hip extension strength and pelvic and spinal stability with an emphasis on the crosspattern strength of the glutes, obliques, rear deltoids, and triceps

Equipment

Stability ball and dowel rod

Starting Position

- Lie supine on a stability ball with the ball under the shoulder blades, head resting on the ball, hips extended, and heels right under the knees and just outside shoulder width.
- Hold a dowel rod across the chest perpendicular to the body with the hands supine and elbows extended.

Procedure

- Take a step with the right foot moving it next to the left.
- Step to the left with the left foot, keeping the feet parallel and toes pointed forward.
- Slide the upper body laterally over the ball until the sternum lines up with the center of the pelvis.
- Hold for 3 seconds; then return to the starting position.
- During the hold, make sure the hips are extended and the pelvis is level.
- Repeat on the right.

Stability Ball Hip Extension and Knee Flexion

Purpose

To develop strength in hip extension and knee flexion with a primary emphasis on glute and hamstring strength

Equipment

Stability ball

Starting Position

- Lie supine on the floor with the heels on and over the center of the stability ball.
- Abduct the arms perpendicular to the torso and extend the elbows to help balance.
- Extend the hips, creating a straight line from the ankles to the shoulders (figure 8.3a).

Procedure

- Pull the ball in toward the butt by flexing at the knees (figure 8.3b).

Figure 8.3 Stability ball hip extension and knee flexion: *(a)* starting position; *(b)* bring the ball in toward the butt.

- Keep the hips extended, maintaining a straight line from the knees to the shoulders throughout the exercise.
- Return to the starting position with hips extended and repeat.

Variation

To increase difficulty, perform this exercise with one leg instead of two.

CORE STABILITY

Spinal segmental and pelvic stability are key to building a base of core strength. Exercises to build core stability focus on maintaining a posture during isometric holds and movements. Exercise progression begins with lying prone or supine with a solid base of support to learn proper muscle activation. The next step is to decrease the base of support to tax the core, making it resist movement in multiple planes. Finally, exercises should progress to a standing position to work the core in a functional total-body movement pattern.

LA Coordination

Purpose

To develop lower abdominal activation and strength

Starting Position

- Lie supine on the floor with the hands underneath the low back above the PSIS (posterior superior iliac spine).
- Flex the hips and knees so the upper legs are perpendicular to the floor and the heels are pulled in tight to the backs of the legs.
- Dorsiflex the ankles.

Procedure

- Posteriorly rotate the pelvis, applying pressure into the hands.
- While maintaining pressure on the hands, lower the left heel. Lightly touch it to the floor and return to the starting position (figure 8.4a).
- Repeat with the right heel (figure 8.4b).
- Keep the stationary leg vertical. Bringing the knee toward the head reduces the effort of the lower abdominals to stabilize the pelvis.

Figure 8.4 LA coordination: (a) lightly touch left heel to floor; (b) lightly touch right heel to floor.

Note

To increase exercise difficulty, extend the knee to increase the angle between the upper and lower leg.

Front Plank

Purpose

To develop core stability with a primary emphasis on the front abdominals.

Starting Position

Lie supine on the floor.

Procedure

- Place the forearms on the floor, elbows directly under the shoulders.
- Place the feet together on the floor with the bottoms of the feet perpendicular to the floor.
- Position the torso so the tailbone is the same height as the shoulder blades.
- Slightly posteriorly rotate the pelvis to activate the lower abdominals and place the spine in a neutral position.
- Push the elbows into the floor to slightly elevate the body through the shoulder joints. (This creates scapular stability.)
- Hold this position (figure 8.5) for the prescribed amount of time.

Figure 8.5   Front plank.

Note

Increase the difficulty of this exercise by placing the shoulders behind the elbows.

Side Plank

Purpose

To develop core stability with a primary emphasis on the lateral hip and lateral abdominals

Starting Position

Lie on the left side on the floor.

Procedure

- With the torso perpendicular to the floor, place the right forearm on the floor with the elbow directly under the shoulder.
- Place the right side of the foot on the floor, and evert the foot to lift the ankle off the floor.
- Place the left hand on the left hip.
- Lift the left hip as high as possible.
- Push the elbow into the floor to slightly elevate the body through the shoulder joint and squeeze the scapulae together. (This creates scapular stability.)
- Hold this position (figure 8.6) for the prescribed amount of time.
- Repeat on the opposite side.

Figure 8.6 Side plank.

Note

Maintain postural alignment throughout to keep the top shoulder from rolling forward or the hips from drifting forward or back.

Side Plank With Leg Abduction

Purpose

To develop core stability with a primary emphasis on the lateral hip and lateral abdominals

Starting Position

Get into position for a side plank on the right forearm.

Procedure

- Keeping the knee straight, abduct the left leg, lifting it in the air (figure 8.7).
- Be sure to keep the outside of the left foot facing up and the left leg directly over the right leg.
- After reaching the maximal range of motion, return to the starting position and repeat. Repeat with the left forearm on the floor and abduct the right leg.

Figure 8.7   Side plank with leg abduction.

Slide Board Mountain Climber

Purpose

To develop multiplane core stability with a primary emphasis on the hip flexors, front and lateral abdominals, and glutes

Equipment

Slide board and slide board boots

Setup

Place a slide board on the floor and put on slide board booties.

Starting Position

- Place the feet on the slide board with the soles perpendicular to the floor.
- Place the hands on the floor in front of the slide board and directly under the shoulders.
- Create a tabletop back position by lifting and holding the tailbone level with the shoulder blades.
- Push through the floor so the shoulders are slightly elevated, creating scapular stability.

Procedure

- Lift the left foot off the slide board and flex the hip and knee, pulling the knee toward the chest.
- Extend the left hip and knee and dorsiflex the ankle, creating a straight line from the shoulder to the heel.
- Place the left foot back on the slide board and repeat, alternating left and right.
- Throughout the exercise, maintain the starting position posture.
- Perform slow, controlled movements to lengthen the time under tension.

Note

To increase exercise difficulty, position the shoulders slightly behind the hands.

Bar Rollout

Purpose

To develop core stability and strength

Equipment

Barbell with weights on each end or an ab roller, and a pad to kneel on

Starting Position

Kneel on the pad and grasp the bar with the hands just outside shoulder width with a closed, pronated grip.

Procedure

- Straighten the elbows (but do not lock them out) and externally rotate the humerus by rotating the elbows back (figure 8.8*a*).
- Posteriorly rotate the pelvis.
- Using the knees as a pivot point, lean the body forward and flex the arms at the shoulders to slowly and under control roll the bar out (figure 8.8*b*).
- Keep rolling until the torso and the arms are almost in a straight line or as far as you can go while keeping the low back flat and the hips posteriorly rotated.

Figure 8.8   Bar rollout: *(a)* straighten the elbows; *(b)* roll out the bar.

Side Bend

Purpose

To develop strength in the lateral hip and obliques

Equipment

Side bend bench or glute-ham machine

Starting Position

Get onto the side bend bench with the body in a straight line from the shoulder to the hip and the arms crossed on the chest or with hands behind the ears.

Procedure

- Side bend toward the floor, moving through the abdomen (figure 8.9a).
- Reverse direction and side bend toward the ceiling (figure 8.9b), decreasing the space between the top ASIS and the last rib.
- Throughout the exercise, keep the torso and lower body in the same plane.

Figure 8.9   Side bend: (a) toward the floor; (b) toward the ceiling.

Pallof Press

Purpose

To develop lateral hip and core stability and strength in a standing position

Equipment

Cable column

Setup

Position the handle attachment of the cable column just below the chest.

Starting Position

- Stand perpendicular to the cable machine.
- Grab the cable handle with the far hand first and place the close hand over it.
- Pull the weight off the stack.
- Pull the handle into the chest (figure 8.10a).
- Keep the hips and knees slightly flexed.

Procedure

- Press the handle in front of the chest until the arms are straight but not locked out (figure 8.10b).
- Pause.
- Return to the starting position.

Figure 8.10   Pallof press: (a) starting position; (b) press handle out.

Prone Cobra

Purpose

To develop posterior shoulder, back, and glute strength with an emphasis on the external shoulder rotators, rear deltoids, scapular abductors, thoracic and lumbar extensors, and glutes

Starting Position

Lie prone on the floor.

Procedure

- Lift the chest off the floor by extending through the lumbar and thoracic spine.
- Pull the arms back and up to the ceiling and rotate the thumbs up toward the ceiling (figure 8.11).
- Squeeze the glutes.
- Hold for 3 seconds and return to the starting position.
- Repeat.

Figure 8.11 Prone cobra.

Three-Position Prone Cobra

Purpose

To develop posterior shoulder, back, and glute strength with an emphasis on the external shoulder rotators, rear deltoids, scapular abductors, thoracic and lumbar extensors, and glutes

Starting Position

Lie prone on the floor.

Procedure

Lift the chest off the floor by extending through the lumbar and thoracic spine and squeeze the glutes. Perform repetitions at three arm positions:

- Position 1: Arms out in front at 45-degree angles, shoulders maximally flexed, elbows extended, and thumbs pointed up (figure 8.12a).
- Position 2: Arms perpendicular to the torso, elbows extended, and thumbs pointed up toward the ceiling (figure 8.12b).
- Position 3: Arms pulled back. Squeeze the shoulder blades and rotate the hands back. Point the thumbs toward the ceiling (figure 8.12c).

Figure 8.12   Three-position prone cobra: (a) arms in front; (b) arms perpendicular; (c) arms pulled back.

Prone Cobra Reach and Rotate

Purpose

To develop posterior shoulder, back, and glute strength with an emphasis on the external shoulder rotators, rear deltoids, scapular abductors, thoracic and lumbar extensors, and glutes

Starting Position

Lie prone on the floor.

Procedure

Lift the chest off the floor by extending through the lumbar and thoracic spine and squeeze the glutes. The arms will move in opposite directions.

- Reach the left arm out in front and then pull it up and back. Flex the left shoulder maximally, extend the elbow, and point the thumb up.
- Reach the right arm down toward the hip, elbow extended (figure 8.13).
- Switch right and left arm positions after each repetition.

Figure 8.13   Prone cobra reach and rotate.

CORE POWER

Core power is generated in the preload, eccentric phase, of the movement. This can be observed in the arm swing of hitters who create pace and power on the ball by initiating the attack with their hips while lagging the shoulder and arm back to generate a whiplike motion. Core power training should focus first on proper kinematic sequencing and muscle lengthening before moving to the actual transfer of power in the form of weighted throws. It is important to note that traditional crunch exercises, if done in large volumes, may actually inhibit power production by leaving the muscle in a shortened state and decreasing the body's ability to preload (lengthen) the core and get adequate hip and trunk separation.

▶ Multidirection Weight Plate Shoulder Press

Purpose

- Primary: To eccentrically lengthen the core in three planes of movement
- Secondary: To strengthen the shoulders in multiple planes of movement

Equipment

Weight plate or dumbbells

Starting Position

Stand with feet shoulder-width apart and parallel. Hold the dumbbells at chest height and press the backs of the upper arms against the rib cage.

Procedure

During the shoulder press, keep the heels flat on the floor and extend the elbows. The arms are the driver; let them dictate the movement of the rest of the body. Look at the dumbbells as you press them. Perform the following three pressing movements:

- Front to back: Press both dumbbells up and forward and return to the starting position. Press the dumbbells up and back and return to the starting position.
- Side to side: Press both dumbbells up and to the right; then return to the starting position. Press both dumbbells up and to the left; then return to the starting position.
- Rotate: Press both dumbbells up and over the shoulder to the right; then return to the starting position. Press both dumbbells up and rotate them to the left; then return to the starting position.

Single-Arm Dumbbell Over-the-Shoulder Press

Purpose

- Primary: To eccentrically lengthen the core in rotation
- Secondary: To strengthen the shoulders

Equipment

One dumbbell

Starting Position

Stand with feet shoulder-width apart. Hold a dumbbell in the right hand at shoulder height with the right elbow pointed toward the floor and maximally flexed.

Procedure

- Press the dumbbell over the left shoulder, causing the body to rotate to the left (figure 8.14a). Return to the starting position.
- Press the dumbbell over the right shoulder, causing the body to rotate to the right (figure 8.14b). Return to the starting position.
- Perform the exercise rapidly but under control without any pauses between movements. Repeat, holding the dumbbell in the left hand.

Figure 8.14   Single-arm dumbbell over-the-shoulder press: (a) press dumbbell over left shoulder and rotate to the left; (b) press dumbbell over right shoulder and rotate to the right.

▶ Medicine Ball Chop Toss

Purpose

To develop transverse plane core explosiveness

Equipment

Medicine ball

Starting Position

Stand with feet shoulder-width apart. Hold a medicine ball at the waist.

Procedure

- Swing the medicine ball up and to the right until it is overhead.
- With the ball overhead, initiate the movement by extending and rotating the hips to the left simultaneously crunching the abdominals and tossing the ball down and to the left of the left foot. Grab the ball and repeat.
- Repeat, swinging and tossing the ball from left to right.

Note

The medicine ball moves in a circle from start to finish.

▶ Overhead Medicine Ball Crunch Toss

Purpose

To develop sagittal plane core explosiveness

Equipment

Medicine ball, solid wall to throw the medicine ball against

Starting Position

Stand 10 to 12 feet (3 to 3.7 m) from the wall and face the wall.

Procedure

- Keeping the arms as straight as possible, raise the medicine ball from the waist to overhead.
- As the ball moves overhead, keep the pelvis in a neutral position, moving through the shoulders and upper back.
- At the end range of motion, quickly reverse direction by posteriorly rotating the pelvis and crunching the rib cage down and throwing the ball against the wall.
- This creates a pikelike movement at the abdomen.
- Throw the medicine ball at the wall 6 to 12 inches (15 to 30 cm) from the floor.

▶ Overhead Medicine Ball Oblique Toss

Purpose

To develop sagittal plane core explosiveness

Equipment

Medicine ball, solid wall to throw the medicine ball against

Starting Position

Stand 10 to 12 feet (3 to 3.7 m) from the wall, perpendicular to the wall with the left side closer to the wall.

Procedure

- Move the ball from the left hip in front of the forehead, rotating right and ending with the medicine ball over the right shoulder.
- Initiate the throw by rotating through the hips. Throw the medicine ball at the wall 6 to 12 inches (15 to 30 cm) from the floor.

Overhead Medicine Ball Dribble

Purpose

To develop dynamic core stability

Equipment

Medicine ball, solid wall to throw the medicine ball against

Starting Position

Stand with the toes 3 to 6 inches (7.6 to 15 cm) from the wall.

Procedure

- Hold a medicine ball in both hands overhead.
- Rapidly bounce the ball off the wall (figure 8.15) for the prescribed number of repetitions.
- Maintain a neutral lumbar spine and stable pelvis throughout the drill.

Figure 8.15 Overhead medicine ball dribble.

SHOULDER PREHAB

A volleyball shoulder prehabilitation program should consist of exercises to develop a base of shoulder strength as well as exercises that integrate the thoracic spine, scapulae, and shoulders together in movements opposite of an arm swing while attacking. Traditional shoulder exercises that isolate one movement such as shoulder flexion, abduction, lateral rotation, and external rotation can develop a base of strength. However, a base of strength is not enough. A volleyball arm swing is performed in three dimensions and always involves the core, thoracic spine, and scapulae. Therefore, movements opposite that of the arm swing, such as those for the lateral and external rotators of the shoulder, the rear deltoid, the scapular abductors, and the thoracic spine, should also be addressed.

Ls, Ws, Ys, and Ts

Purpose

To develop lateral deltoid, posterior deltoid, and rotator cuff strength

Equipment

Light dumbbells or weight plates ranging from 2.5 to 10 lbs

Starting Position

- Stand with feet hip-width apart and knees slightly bent.
- Bend forward at the hips, keeping the lumbar spine in a neutral position until the torso is at a 45-degree angle.

Procedure

- Ls: Pull the elbows up to shoulder height, creating a 90-degree angle at the elbow and between the torso and upper arm (figure 8.16*a*). Externally rotate at the shoulder (figure 8.16*b*).

Figure 8.16   Ls.

- Ws: Keep the elbows directly under the shoulders and flex the elbows to 90 degrees (figure 8.17a). Abduct the upper arm, lifting the elbows as high as possible (figure 8.17b).
- Ys: Keeping the thumbs up and elbows straight (figure 8.18a), maximally flex the shoulder, lifting the arms toward the ceiling and ending in a V position (figure 8.18b).
- Ts: Keeping the thumbs up and elbows straight (figure 8.19a), pull the hands out to the sides, performing a reverse fly (figure 8.19b).

Figure 8.17   Ws.

Figure 8.18   Ys.

Figure 8.19   Ts.

Note

Often a lighter weight is used for the Ls and Ws and slightly heavier weights are used for Ys and Ts.

Arm Circle

Purpose

To develop integrated strength of the upper back and shoulders

Starting Position

Stand tall with feet shoulder-width apart. Maximally flex the elbows and place the backs of the lower arms and hands against each other.

Procedure

- Keeping the elbows flexed, maximally flex the shoulders and bring the elbows up and back.
- Perform a half circle with the elbows, pulling them back and down to shoulder height.
- Externally rotate the shoulders, moving the hands back.
- Extend the elbows and pull the arms down while squeezing the scapulae together.
- Pull the arms in front, back to the starting position, and repeat.

Note

Throughout the exercise, focus on maxing out the range of motion of the elbows. This creates the resistance of the exercise and promotes proper thoracic spine and shoulder mobility.

SUMMARY

Functional core training focuses on stabilizing or transferring energy through the torso to connect the upper and lower body. The ability to stabilize and transfer energy is vital when performing an explosive arm swing or making powerful motions with the lower body while maintaining relaxed control of the upper body to make defensive plays on a ball. To model and train real-life movements, exercises should focus on glute activation, spinal stability, eccentric loading of the abdominals, and the integration of the core and the shoulder, not isolated movements such as the traditional crunch or rotator cuff exercises.

Chapter 9

Conditioning

In volleyball, maintaining quickness and power during a rally or set and throughout an entire match is vital to maximize performance. The average rally in Division I NCAA women's volleyball lasts 13 seconds, but rallies commonly last 30 seconds and, on rare occasions, can be as long as 60 seconds. Movements performed in a rally are interval based, alternating among quick power movements (jumping, diving, accelerating in an approach or to the ball), controlled movements to reposition (shuffling or backpedaling), and periods of waiting to react to the ball in go posture. Rest time between points can last from 10 to 30 seconds, depending on how quickly the ball gets back to the server, how much time someone takes to serve the ball, and whether there are any substitutions. Time-outs can account for 60 to 90 additional seconds between rallies.

Conditioning for volleyball should focus first on developing a solid base of general conditioning and then gradually increase both changes of direction and jumping. A progression to more volleyball-specific interval-based conditioning should be the next step after obtaining a solid base. Aerobic, steady-state conditioning, such as jogging, should be avoided because it trains the energy system that is opposite the one used in volleyball and can diminish the explosive characteristics of muscle.

CONDITIONING BASE

Developing a base of conditioning before moving to volleyball-specific court conditioning is essential to prevent overtraining, provide adequate recovery to allow gains in strength and power, and reduce injuries. The amount of time spent in the base conditioning phase depends on the time of year and the conditioning level of the athlete. The base conditioning phase is implemented in the first of the two off-season training phases, which occur at the beginning of the spring and summer semesters.

The women's collegiate volleyball season can last 16 to 20 weeks, followed by four weeks of winter break. At the University of Illinois, this break is used to unload the athletes. Usually, athletes are given the first two weeks completely off followed by two weeks of light, low-volume training focused on getting them active again. During this time, to unload their joints and promote recovery, they do not jump or perform quick changes of direction. Because the main goal over break is mental and physical recovery and the volume of activity is very light, the athletes return to school not ready to perform high-volume, high-intensity volleyball-specific training. Therefore, the base conditioning phase that takes place at the beginning of the spring semester starts light and gradually increases the exercise intensity and volume of both cutting and ground contacts from jumping exercises. This progression prepares the athletes for a rigorous four- to five-week volleyball-specific training period to get them in shape for the spring competition season.

The base conditioning phase during the first summer semester is identical to the exercises performed during the beginning of the spring. The reasoning for implementing the same exercises is different. In the beginning of the spring semester, the athletes were not physically prepared after time off for intense sport-specific conditioning. In the summer, the base conditioning phase is implemented to unload them from the jumping and cutting exercises that stress the joints, while maintaining a base of conditioning. This base phase lasts approximately four weeks and is followed by volleyball-specific conditioning drills during the second summer semester to prepare them for the demands of the preseason and competitive season to come.

20/10

Purpose

To develop a base of conditioning while performing low-intensity interval training

Procedure

The drill is performed with a continuous clock. When the clock starts, you have 20 seconds to cover a specified distance and then 10 seconds off before repeating for the prescribed amount of time, as follows:

- 120 to 130 feet (37 to 40 m) there and back (total 240 to 260 ft, or 74 to 80 m) in 5 minutes. Rest 120 to 150 seconds.

- 50 to 60 feet (15 to 18 m) there and back twice (total 200 to 240 ft, or 30 to 36 m) in 5 minutes. Rest 120 to 150 seconds.
- 20 to 30 feet (6 to 9 m) there and back four times (total 160 to 240 ft, or 48 to 72 m) in 5 minutes.

▶ Timed Shuffle

Purpose

To develop a base of strength in go posture

Starting Position

Stand in go posture and maintain this posture throughout the drill.

Procedure

- The timed shuffle is performed between the center line and the 10-foot (3 m) line.
- Start in go posture and maintain it throughout the drill. Use good shuffle biomechanics.
- Shuffle between the center line and the 10-foot (3 m) line, covering as much ground as possible in 10 seconds.
- Pair up with another player. One performs the drill and the other sits out, to create a 1:1 work-to-rest ratio.

1-5-1 Sprint Pyramid

Purpose

To introduce change of direction in the base conditioning phase

Procedure

- Pair up with another player and start on the sideline of the court. Alternate participating in the drill and sitting out to create a 1:1 work-to-rest ratio.
- On the coach's command of "Go," sprint across the width of the court, touch your foot on the far sideline, and sprint back to the start. Your partner starts when you cross the start line, sprinting across the court and back.
- When your partner crosses the start line, repeat, sprinting across the court and back twice. This is repeated, partners alternating turns and increasing the distance by one length there and back until you reach five repetitions.

- After you reach five repetitions there and back, work back down, performing four lengths there and back and then reducing each set by one length there and back until you get back to one.

Variations

- 1-3-1 sprint pyramid: This is the same as the 1-5-1 with a reduction in volume. The maximal number of sprints performed is three times there and back.
- 1-4-1 sprint pyramid: This is the same as the 1-5-1 with a reduction in volume. The maximal number of sprints performed is four times there and back.
- Jump 1-5-1 sprint pyramid: This variation is performed like the 1-5-1 sprint pyramid but with the addition of squat jumps for height prior to each sprint. The number of jumps is the same as the number of sprints performed. For example, start with one squat jump and one sprint of the court width there and back. Midway through the drill, perform five squat jumps prior to five sprints of the court width there and back.

▶ Jump, Shuffle, Jump, Sprint Conditioning

Purpose

To introduce jumps and single-plane changes of direction in multiple movements to transition from base conditioning to position-specific conditioning; occurs during the transition phase of conditioning

Procedure

Pair up with another player. Start on the 10-foot (3 m) line, facing the sideline of the court. Alternate participating in the drill and sitting out to create a 1:1 work-to-rest ratio. On the coach's command of "Go," perform this series:

- Perform three squat jumps for height.
- Shuffle from the 10-foot (3 m) line to the center line and back three times.
- Perform three squat jumps for height.
- Sprint from the 10-foot (3 m) line to the opposite 10-foot (3 m) line and back three times.

Alternate participating in the drill and sitting out, and alternate the direction you are facing to start each repetition.

Perform four or five sets of two repetitions with 20 seconds of extra rest between sets, or perform two sets of four repetitions with 90 to 120 seconds of rest between sets.

Multidirection Jump

Purpose

To introduce multiplane movements and jumps to transition from base conditioning to position-specific conditioning; occurs during the transition phase of conditioning

Setup

Designate three stations on a volleyball court:

- Two stations: 20- by 30-foot (6 by 9 m) space between the 10-foot (3 m) line and the baseline and sidelines
- One station: 20- by 30-foot (6 by 9 m) space between the two 10-foot (3 m) lines and the sidelines

Place a piece of tape in the middle of each of the three areas.

Procedure

Pair up with another player. Partners alternate participating in the drill and sitting out to create a 1:1 work-to-rest ratio. Start on the tape in the center of the station, facing a sideline. On the coach's command of "Go," perform this series:

- Perform three squat jumps for height.
- Shuffle 10 feet (3 m) left and back to the start.
- Sprint 15 feet (4.6 m) forward and backpedal to the start.
- Shuffle 10 feet (3 m) right and back to the start.
- Backpedal 15 feet (4.6 m) and sprint back to the start.
- Repeat.

Perform four sets of two repetitions with 20 to 30 seconds of extra rest between sets, or perform two sets of three or four repetitions with 90 to 120 seconds of rest between sets.

VOLLEYBALL-SPECIFIC COURT CONDITIONING

To prepare volleyball players for the rigors of the sport, conditioning must match or exceed the demands they will experience on the court. Volleyball is an interval-based sport consisting of quick or powerful movements combined with controlled movements to reposition oneself or, if in go posture, waiting to react to the ball. Because of the small court area covered and the need to perform quick, powerful movements, volleyball-specific conditioning resembles agility and plyometric exercises or a combination of the two. The primary difference is that in volleyball-specific conditioning, the duration or distance traveled is greater and rest time is shorter than in agility and plyometric training. Work-to-rest ratios can go from 0.5:1 to 2:1 depending on the goal of the drill, when it is performed in the training phase, and the conditioning level of the athlete. Remember, the goal is to be able to jump as high and move as quickly in the fifth set as in the first set. During a conditioning session, if the athletes cannot move at a decent pace or have a marked difference in jump height from the beginning to the end of the drill, they are actually working against the goal of being explosive throughout a match. For this reason, the work-to-rest ratio must be designed so that athletes can work at a high intensity during each drill and throughout the entire conditioning session.

▶ Position Threes

Purpose

To develop position-specific court conditioning

Procedure

This drill is performed in groups of three to establish a 1:2 work-to-rest ratio. The whole series is completed before the next athlete is in the drill.

Attacker Threes

- Perform three approaches and attacks with quick transitions.
- Perform 3 × 3 shuffles there and back.
- Perform three block jumps.
- Backpedal and sprint from the net to the 10-foot (3 m) line and back three times.
- Finish by sprinting from the net through the end line.

Middle Threes

- Perform three approaches and attacks with quick transitions.
- Perform 3 × 3 shuffles there and back.
- Perform three Mikan drill jumps right and three left. The Mikan drill is a layup basketball drill with movements that are very similar to those performed in a slide attack. Start the drill by standing with the left side closer to the net and the body perpendicular to the net. Take a quick step with the left foot while rapidly flexing the right hip and knee and reaching as high as possible with the right hand. Land, turn the hips, and step with the right foot. Flex the left hip and knee and reach as high as possible with the left hand. Repeat for the prescribed number of repetitions.
- Backpedal and sprint from the net to the 10-foot (3 m) line and back three times.
- Perform three block jumps.

Setter Threes

- Perform three block jumps.
- Perform 3×3 shuffles there and back.
- Perform three block jumps.
- Backpedal and sprint from the net to the 10-foot (3 m) line and back three times.
- Finish by sprinting from the net through the end line.

Defense Power Threes

- Perform three broad jumps forward; then backpedal to the start.
- Perform three lateral squats and bounds to the left and shuffle right to the start.
- Perform three lateral squats and bounds to the right and shuffle left to the start.
- Perform three right and three left back-angle speedskaters and sprint back to the start.

Position Repetitions

Purpose

To develop position-specific conditioning

Procedure

This drill is performed with two partners to establish a 1:2 work-to-rest ratio. Partners alternate after each segment.

Attacker

- Approach and transition 5 to 10 times.
- Shuffle block 5 to 10 right, 5 to 10 left.
- Block jump 5 to 10 times.
- Perform the multidirection agility (short) drill twice.

Middle

- Approach and transition 5 to 10 times.
- Swing block 5 to 10 times.
- Perform three shuffle blocks 5 to 10 times.
- Block jump 5 to 10 times.

Setter

- Shuffle block 5 to 10 right, 5 to 10 left.
- Block jump 5 to 10 times.

- Perform the multidirection agility (short) drill 2 to 5 times.
- Court width sprints there and back 3 to 8 times.

Defense

- Multidirection agility (short) 2 to 5 times.
- Shuffle 10 feet (3 m) and back 5 to 8 times.
- Sprint and backpedal 10 feet (3 m) 5 to 8 times.
- Court width sprints there and back 5 to 8 times.

IN-SEASON CONDITIONING

Conditioning must continue in-season to maintain work capacity throughout competition. A specific in-season program for conditioning is not provided here because of the large number of variables that must be considered during program design. A coach must consider the number of sets played in a given week or time period, the number of jumps per athlete, the amount each athlete has competed, and the overall health and fitness of the team members. Conditioning may be different for starters and nonstarters. Usually, in-season conditioning for athletes who play a lot is short but intense (such as suicides) and does not include jumping because of the high number of jumps they perform in a week. Nonstarters, or redshirt athletes, may perform more sprint conditioning and some jump conditioning depending on the volume they receive in practice.

In-season, most coaches maintain players' court conditioning by performing up-tempo, short-rest drills that tax their work capacity in an actual volleyball environment. The key to in-season conditioning is to take a close look at all the variables that affect work capacity and then to design and implement a program with just enough volume to maintain conditioning but not so much that overtraining occurs.

SUMMARY

The ability to jump high and move quickly throughout a set or match is critical to overall performance in volleyball. In the off-season, athletes must first develop a base of conditioning either to prepare for more intense on-court training or to reduce the volume of training (i.e., changes of direction and jumping) to promote healthy joints and recovery. After a conditioning base is achieved, more volleyball-specific conditioning should occur to prepare athletes for the physical demands of in-season training and competition. In-season conditioning is based on the team and individual athlete's needs. The goal of in-season conditioning is to perform just enough of a stimulus to maintain conditioning levels without overstressing the athletes and reducing performance.

Part III

TRAINING PROGRAMS

Year-round training is essential to maximize physical development in volleyball players. It is important to focus on individual and team goals, include each component of training during each phase of training, and properly progress both exercises and exercise volume. When designing training programs, coaches and athletes should do the following:

- Focus on the goals of the program. If the goals are to increase power production and decrease injuries, every component of training and the program implemented should address those goals.
- Make sure all components of training are addressed in relation to the needs specific to volleyball.
- Develop a progressive training program that teaches or refreshes technique, minimizes plateaus, and eliminates overuse injuries.

The upcoming chapters discuss off-season and in-season training and provide sample programs for both. Before diving into the training programs, we address the components of programs as well as plyometric and agility nomenclature. This will aid in your understanding of the focus, correct execution, and progression of the exercises presented in the upcoming programs.

PROGRAM COMPONENTS

The four standard program components are tempo, rest, volume, and intensity. Each must be clearly defined for the coach and athlete to understand the expectations of each drill or exercise as well as to maximize the desired benefit.

Tempo is the speed of each movement in an exercise. Tempo is designated with a three-digit number separated by dashes, or with the cues *hold, C, Q,* or *E.* The first number in the three-digit sequence indicates the speed of the first movement. The second number designates a transition of movement or a pause. The third number indicates the speed of the final movement. All numbers represent time in seconds. For example, a back squat with a tempo of 3-1-1 signifies a 3-second descent into the squat, a 1-second pause at the bottom, and then a 1-second ascent. A tempo of *hold 30* would be an isometric hold of 30 seconds. *C* indicates that the exercise is performed in a controlled fashion and is typically used when multiple movements are executed within one repetition. *Q* indicates that the athlete should move as quickly as possible throughout the entire movement. *E* represents an explosive movement with the focus being to move the body, an implement, or a bar as rapidly as possible.

Rest is the amount of time given to recover between sets or exercises. Rest time is important because it can dictate the load or intensity at which an athlete is able to work, the physiological adaptations of the body as a result of the exercise, and the level of muscle soreness and physical fatigue posttraining. Longer rest times should be used with explosive lifts, high-intensity strength training (high percentage of 1-repetition maximum, or 1RM), agility training, and plyometrics. Rest can be measured by time on a clock or can be built into the exercise naturally by placing the athletes in groups. For example, a group of four athletes on a platform, at a squat rack, or at an agility or plyometric station automatically creates a 1:3 work-to-rest ratio.

Volume equals the number of sets multiplied by the number of repetitions in a given session, week, or cycle. It can also be defined as the number of jumps or floor contacts, the number of direction changes in agility or conditioning drills, or the total running distance covered in a drill.

Intensity is the percentage of the athlete's 1RM or projected 1RM. An intensity of 100 percent represents the load that can be lifted with good technique only once. An athlete's 1RM can be projected based on the load lifted using more repetitions. This estimated 1RM can be used to prescribe weights for the athlete.

CATEGORIZING MOVEMENT FOR PLYOMETRIC AND AGILITY EXERCISES

Plyometric and agility exercises can be executed and progressed in a variety of ways. The following nomenclature is used to describe the focus of the exercises and how they should be implemented.

Plyometrics

Singles: Repetitions within a set that are performed individually. The athlete resets to the proper starting position before performing the next repetition.

Stick: Performing one explosive effort with an emphasis on proper biomechanical alignment upon landing. The landing position is held for 2 seconds before the athlete resets to the starting position or rests between repetitions.

Pause: Performing multiple sticks within a repetition sequence. A pause is implemented to work on proper landing mechanics or to reset to the proper starting position prior to performing the next repetition within a repetition range.

Counter: Performing a second movement in the opposite direction without pausing after the first movement. For example, while performing a lateral squat and bound, the athlete bounds to the left, sinks into a squat, and immediately bounds back to the right. When performing a countermovement, the athlete remains in motion until the second movement is complete. During the landing phase of the first movement, the athlete sinks down into a squat to decelerate upon landing and then immediately accelerates out of the squat in the opposite direction.

Continuous (Cont.): Performing all repetitions in succession.

Acceleration and Agility

Singles: Single-plane movements; accelerating from point A to point B.

Pause: Resetting in go posture after each repetition. The coach initiates each repetition to make sure go posture is achieved and to better observe and teach proper acceleration biomechanics to multiple athletes at one time. The primary reason for implementing a pause is to work on the acceleration out of go posture.

Continuous (Cont.): Performing all repetitions or changes of direction in succession.

Mirror: Shadowing the movements of another athlete.

React singles: Reacting to a visual stimulus and travel a predetermined distance.

React doubles: Reacting to a visual stimulus to start the drill and reacting to a second visual stimulus to change direction.

React reps: Reacting to a visual stimulus to initiate the drill and move from point A to point B and back to the starting position. Upon returning to the starting position, the athlete resets in go posture before performing another repetition.

React continuous: Reacting to a visual stimulus to start the drill. Throughout the drill, multiple visual stimuli (representing repetitions) initiate changes of direction.

Chapter 10

Mobility Program Design and Implementation

Implementing a well-designed mobility program can help improve or maintain range of motion, promote recovery between sessions, and decrease injuries. This chapter outlines some basic principles for designing and implementing mobility programs and provides program examples.

PROGRAM DESIGN

Mobility programs can be designed based on information obtained from an individual assessment, described in chapter 1, or can be generalized based on the needs of the sport. A program design based on an assessment is focused on an athlete's particular mobility needs. Appropriate releases, mobility exercises and stretches, and volumes can be prescribed to more immediately reduce any muscle imbalances or immobilities.

The assessment also can be used in a broader way to evaluate the team as a whole. For instance, the most common joint restrictions I have found in volleyball players are ankle dorsiflexion, thoracic extension, shoulder flexion, and shoulder internal rotation. If most of the athletes within a team have immobility or imbalance issues, exercises to address these issues can be incorporated into a general program for all team members.

Developing an Individualized Program

An individualized program based on the assessments in chapter 1 should include the myofascial releases, mobility exercises, and stretches presented in chapter 3. Each test indicates the specific release, mobility exercise, or stretch that should be prescribed for those with positive results. The volume is based on the severity of the restriction. Remedying significant imbalances between the left and right sides should be the first priority when designing an individualized program because of their negative effects on posture and joint biomechanics and the increased susceptibility to injury they cause compared to bilateral tightness. When a left-to-right imbalance is present, volume should be twice as much for the tighter side. If one side is tight and the other is at optimal range, the nonrestricted muscle or joint should not be stretched until both sides are equal.

Developing a General Program

A general mobility program is designed around the basic needs of volleyball players. Although such a program can be productive, it can be limited in its ability to remedy muscle imbalances from left to right and lack the necessary volume to address some athletes' mobility issues. With myofascial releases or stretches, the time under tension for each body part should be a minimum of 30 seconds and a maximum of 2 minutes. The longer the hold is, the more likely the muscle will be to relax and elongate. The more severe the tightness or unhealthy the tissue, the higher the volume and frequency needed to get results.

IMPLEMENTATION

The sequence of modalities and the timing—pretraining, during training, or posttraining—are critical to optimize results and get the most benefits from a training session. Pretraining myofascial releases, joint mobilizations, and dynamic stretches are used to increase tissue pliability, gain joint range of motion, wake up proprioceptors, and activate muscles. Posttraining myofascial release techniques and static and proprioceptive neuromuscular facilitation (PNF) stretching are performed to help with tissue recovery and increase muscle flexibility. Static and PNF stretching are not recommended pretraining or during training or competition because they are associated with a small period of decreased power output after they are implemented.

If immobility affects a particular exercise in a training session, the joint should be mobilized before the exercise is performed. For example, an athlete with a deficit in shoulder flexion should mobilize it prior to performing a snatch exercise. This will allow her to freely catch the bar overhead, potentially increasing the weight she can lift and decreasing stress, strain, and the chance of injury of the shoulder and the back. An athlete with a deficit in ankle dorsiflexion should mobilize her ankle prior to practice, agility training, or squatting in the weight room. A deficit in ankle dorsiflexion can reduce an athlete's ability to decelerate load in the landing phase of a jump and decrease the ability to create efficient angles in go posture and when squatting. This will result in decreased speed, quickness, and reaction time on the court. It will also reduce the ability to reach a full range of motion in a squat, create plateaus in weight lifted during a squat, and increase stress on the knees and back while squatting.

The modality order within a program can have a dramatic effect on program results. The pretraining modality order should be myofascial releases, joint mobilizations, and dynamic stretching. The postworkout order should be myofascial releases followed by static or PNF stretching. Fascia covers muscles, joints, and bones. Improving the pliability of this soft tissue will improve the ability of the muscle to lengthen and the joint to move. As a result, the joints will work more efficiently.

DYNAMIC WARM-UP

Every session, whether physical training, practice, or competition, should start with a dynamic warm-up. The goal of a dynamic warm-up is to elevate core temperature, increase range of motion, increase neural muscle activation, and mentally focus the athlete for the task at hand. Two dynamic warm-up programs are presented in tables 10.1 and 10.2. Program 1 is implemented prior to posterior chain–dominant lift days (jump shrug, snatch); program 2 is implemented prior to anterior chain–dominant days (squat, box step-up).

Table 10.1   Dynamic Warm-Up 1

Exercise	Volume	Page number
Myofascial release for calves, hamstrings, hips, glutes, and posterior shoulders	4 minutes total	48-55
Movement: court width	3×	206
Three-plane ankle mob	10	56
Hand walkout with three-plane reach	3×	62
Spiderman crawl	3×	63
Lunge and twist	3×	62
Lateral squat	5×	64
Cross behind and reach	2	65
Forward plyo skip	45 feet (14 m)	208
Backward plyo skip	45 feet (14 m)	208
Lateral plyo skip	45 feet (14 m), moving left and right	209

Table 10.2 Dynamic Warm-Up 2

Exercise	Volume	Page number
Myofascial release for IT band, lateral quad, rectus femoris, and groin	4 minutes total	48-55
Movement: court lines	2×	206
Standing ankle mob (wall)	8	57
Box hip flexor 1	5	66
Box hip flexor 2	8	68
Wide stance groin	8	65
TFL/IT band	5	69
Forward plyo skip	2× court width	208
Backward plyo skip	2× court width	208
Lateral plyo skip	2× court width	209

Movement: Court Width

Starting Position

Stand on the court sideline.

Procedure

Perform each movement across the width of the court and back twice. The intensity should be low, but proper biomechanics should be used.

- Jog across and backpedal back.
- Shuffle across and shuffle back.
- Carioca across and carioca back. Carioca moving right is performed by alternating moving the left foot in front of and then behind the right foot while the right foot shuffle steps. The drill is then repeated moving left with the right foot alternating in front of and behind the left foot.
- Forward skip across and backward skip back.

Movement: Court Lines

Starting Position

Stand in one corner of the court.

Procedure

- Shuffle to the right across the end line (figure 10.1).
- Backpedal to the 10-foot (3 m) line.

- Shuffle to the left across the 10-foot (3 m) line.
- Backpedal to the center line.
- Shuffle to the right across the court.
- Backpedal to the 10-foot (3 m) line.
- Shuffle to the left across the court.
- Backpedal to the end line.
- Shuffle to the right across the court.
- Jog quickly from the end line to the opposite end line.
- Repeat, going in the opposite direction and finishing at the start.

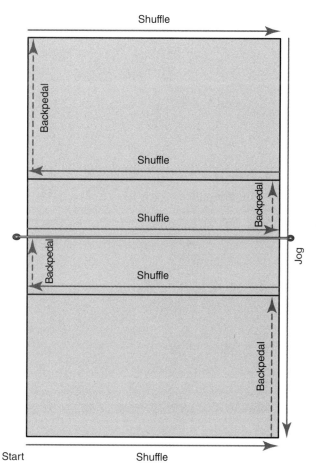

Figure 10.1 Movement: court lines.

▶ Forward Plyo Skip

Starting Position

Stand on the sideline facing the court.

Procedure

- Simultaneously flex the hip and knee and dorsiflex the ankle of the left leg while flexing the right shoulder with the elbow bent at 90 degrees.
- Drive the left forefoot into the floor, extending at the hip, knee, and ankle and driving the body up and forward.
- As the left leg drives down to the floor, the right hip, knee, and ankle flex, the left arm flexes at the shoulder, and the right arm extends at the shoulder.
- The skip is achieved because each foot contacts the floor twice before transitioning to the other leg, aiding in the rhythm of the exercise.
- Throughout the exercise, the arm movement comes from the shoulder and the elbow remains flexed at 90 degrees.

Note

It is important to flex the hip and knee so that the thigh is parallel to the floor. This gives adequate range of motion to apply force into the floor.

Coaching Points

- Focus on driving the forefoot into the floor and getting full extension of the hip, knee, and ankle.
- Achieve enough height on the skip to pause in the air before transitioning to the next leg.

▶ Backward Plyo Skip

Starting Position

Stand on the sideline facing away from the court.

Procedure

- Simultaneously flex the hip and knee and dorsiflex the ankle of the left leg while flexing the right shoulder with the elbow bent at 90 degrees.
- Drive the left forefoot into the floor, extending at the hip, knee, and ankle to drive the body up and backward.

- As the left leg drives down to the floor, the right hip, knee, and ankle flex, the left arm flexes at the shoulder, and the right arm extends at the shoulder.
- The skip is achieved because each foot contacts the floor twice before transitioning to the other leg, aiding in the rhythm of the exercise.
- Throughout the exercise, the arm movement comes from the shoulder and the elbow remains flexed at 90 degrees.

Coaching Points

- Focus on driving the forefoot into the floor and getting full extension of the hip, knee, and ankle.
- Keep the shoulders over the hips. Do not allow the shoulders to move forward when flexing the hip and knee.
- It is important to flex the hip and knee so that the thigh is parallel to the floor. This gives adequate range of motion to apply force into the floor.
- Achieve enough height on the skip to pause in the air before transitioning to the next leg.

▶ Lateral Plyo Skip

Starting Position

Stand perpendicular to the sideline with the right side nearer the court.

Procedure

- Flex the hip and knee and dorsiflex the ankle while crossing the left leg in front of the right.
- Drive the inside portion of the forefoot (the joint connecting the big toe to the foot) into the floor, extending at the hip, knee, and ankle and propelling the body to the right.
- As the left leg drives down to the floor, the right leg shuffle steps to the right.
- The skip is achieved because each foot contacts the floor twice before transitioning to the other leg, aiding in the rhythm of the exercise.
- Perform the exercise moving to the right and then to the left.

Coaching Points

- Focus on driving the inside forefoot into the floor and getting full extension of the hip, knee, and ankle.
- Focus on traveling laterally as opposed to getting height.

GENERAL RECOVERY PROGRAM

A recovery program is performed after training or practice or on days off to promote tissue health and recovery and to maintain or gain flexibility. The general program outlined in table 10.3 focuses on muscles that commonly become tight and can impair volleyball performance. A general program is best for large groups when individual assessments have not been performed. An athlete who has had an individual assessment can perform the general myofascial releases indicated here to sustain total-body muscle health but should focus on correcting her own deficiencies or imbalances to optimize her performance and reduce the potential for injury.

Table 10.3 General Recovery Program

Myofascial release	Time under tension	Page number
Plantar fascia release	30 seconds	48
Calf and Achilles tendon	30 seconds	48
Hamstring release	30 seconds	52
IT band	30 seconds	51
Lateral quad release	30 seconds	50
Piriformis release	30 seconds	53
Rectus femoris release	30 seconds	50
Hamstring muscle origin	30 seconds	52
Latissimus dorsi and teres major release	30 seconds	54
Posterior shoulder and scapula release	30 seconds	55
Stretches	**Time under tension**	**Page number**
Half-kneeling psoas stretch with band	60 seconds	75
Rectus femoris stretch	2 × 30 seconds	72
Forearm to instep complex	15/15/15/15 seconds	78
PNF standing piriformis stretch	2 repetitions each position	77
Three-position groin rock	15/15/15 seconds	76
PNF standing shoulder flexion	4 to 6 repetitions	79
Sleeper stretch (dominant hand)	30 seconds	81
Straight-leg calf stretch	30 seconds	71
Bent-knee calf stretch	30 seconds	72

SUMMARY

A plan to maintain or improve mobility is necessary for optimizing performance and preventing injury. A mobility program, whether general for a team or individualized based on athlete assessment, will help volleyball players meet these goals.

Chapter 11

Off-Season Programs

The off-season is the time to maximize physical development. Lack of or limited competition allows for higher volumes of training. A four-day training program is recommended so that each component of training can be implemented multiple times throughout a training week. Training components of balance, stability, strength, power, foot quickness, acceleration, and agility are not separated into different sessions. Rather, they are performed in every session or every other session. Training each component every (or every other) session helps reinforce proper drill and exercise technique, coordinate movement patterns, and provide adequate stimulus for the body to adapt and improve performance.

The sample off-season program outlined in this chapter has been methodically designed to enable athletes to maximize benefits within a session, recover from session to session, and properly progress exercises and intensity.

EXERCISE SEQUENCE WITHIN A SESSION

A comprehensive program containing all training components in each session requires proper exercise sequencing and distribution to maximize performance and promote recovery. Following is a recommended sequence:

1. **Quick feet:** These activities are performed first because they are the least stressful to the body, are great extensions of the preworkout dynamic warm-up, and wake up the neuromuscular system to facilitate quick, coordinated movements.

2. **Plyometrics:** These drills are performed second to maximize the velocity on each repetition or effort. Plyometrics are overexaggerated, foundational movements of acceleration and deceleration. These movements are performed prior to the more complex movements found in agility drills.

3. **Agility drills:** Maximal effort, attention to proper body mechanics, and maximal recovery are essential for developing proper movement patterns and eliciting enough of a stimulus to increase acceleration and quickness. If agility drills are performed after weight training, the focus on movement mechanics will deteriorate and the stimulus will not be significant enough to allow for adaption.

4. **Resisted power exercises:** Multijoint power exercises such as snatch, clean, jump shrug, and VertiMax exercises should be performed next to ensure maximal power output. At this point, the athlete is properly warmed up, the fast-twitch muscle fibers are firing, and the neuromuscular system has be activated following plyometrics or the quick accelerations or changes of direction in agility drills. The body has been primed to move weight quickly.

5. **Big-muscle multijoint strength exercises:** These exercises are next to maximize force production. Big-muscle multijoint exercises severely fatigue the athlete's neuromuscular, muscular, and endocrine systems. If they are performed prior to any of the four previous exercises, performance would be significantly inhibited. These exercises include the back squat, front squat, RDL, deadlift, box step-up, and lunge.

6. **Smaller-muscle multijoint strength exercises:** Usually, these exercises are performed with a lighter load than multijoint exercises. Examples include the row, push-up, and shoulder press.

7. **Core exercises:** The question of where to place core exercises within a program is a gray area. Exercises focused on core stability performed in prone and supine positions usually are performed after multijoint exercises, but there are some exceptions. I place plank exercises prior to exercises that cause extreme fatigue in the shoulders to ensure that the core is stressed rather than the shoulders. Core exercises in a standing position are full-body multijoint exercises and can be placed prior to smaller-muscle multijoint strength exercises. Plyometric core training should be performed with other plyometric exercises early in the workout so they can be performed at a high velocity and in an unfatigued state.

8. **Single-joint exercises:** These exercises, such as Ls, Ws, Ys, and Ts, are performed last because they fatigue a single muscle or joint, which compromises the athlete's ability to perform multijoint strength exercises. For example, fatiguing the shoulders prior to performing push-ups will inhibit performance or reduce the total number of push-ups achieved.

EXERCISE DISTRIBUTION WITHIN A TRAINING WEEK

The four-day program outlined here (tables 11.1 to 11.6) has training days on Monday, Tuesday, Thursday, and Friday. Exercises must be distributed appropriately throughout the week to achieve maximal performance, promote recovery, and reduce the incidence of overuse injuries because training is performed on back-to-back days twice during the week.

Lifting is divided into hip, chest, and shoulder–dominant exercises on Monday and Thursday and quad and back–dominant movements on Tuesday and Friday. This division of movements and muscle groups diminishes the negative or fatigue effect of back-to-back lifts.

Abdominal training is broken up, alternating the emphasis between front abs (rectus abdominis) and lateral abs (obliques) on back-to-back days. This format allows adequate recovery from day to day making it possible to train the abs every day.

In the early stages of plyometrics, drills can be broken down into vertical and horizontal or lateral movements (jumping versus bounding). These changes in movement patterns place different stresses and sheer forces on the joints, connective tissues, and muscles. The small variations in movement patterns and joint angles help with recovery from session to session.

In the early stages of acceleration, agility and reaction training movements can be broken down into sagittal and lateral movements. The sagittal plane relates to forward sprinting, pivoting and sprinting, and backpedaling. The lateral plane relates to side-to-side sprinting, cutting, and shuffling by separating the exercises performed on back-to-back workout days by the planes of movement, different movement patterns, joint angles, and joint sheer forces are placed upon the body, which promotes recovery from session to session.

Prior to undertaking a workout, athletes should perform a proper dynamic warm-up as well as any needed individual mobilizations so they can perform workout movements properly. Conditioning (table 11.7) should be performed postlifting on Tuesday and Friday to maximize the strength and power benefits of the exercise program. This allows for one or two days for the athlete to recover before the next workout session.

To maximize recovery, myofascial release techniques, mobilizations, stretching, or yoga should be performed on Wednesday and Saturday or Sunday.

Table 11.1   Off-Season Program: Weeks 1 and 2

MONDAY

Plyometrics, agility, quick feet					
Exercise	**Type**	**Rest**	**Sets × reps**	**Distance**	**Page number**
Agility ladder		Team	1		142
Multidirection squat and bound	Stick	Three per group	2 × 3		125
Backpedal intervals	Pause	Four per group	1L, 1R	10/10/10/10	149
Forward acceleration	Single	Four per group	2L, 2R	20	151

Lifts					
Exercise	**Tempo**	**Rest**	**Sets × reps**	**Intensity**	**Page number**
Jump shrug from floor	E	120	3 × 4	75, 82.5, 87.5	116
Single-arm, single-leg RDL	3-1-1	30	2 × 8		88
Single-arm cable push	2-1-2	60	2 × 10		93
Front plank	Hold	30	4 to 6 × 30 sec		173
Multidirection weight plate shoulder press	1-1-1	60	2 × 8		183
Arm circle	C	No	1 × 8		189

TUESDAY

Plyometrics, agility, quick feet					
Exercise	**Type**	**Rest**	**Sets × reps**	**Distance**	**Page number**
Line hops series, two-feet variation	Cont.	Three per group	1 × 8 sec each		134
Hurdle hop (two legs)	Cont.	Team	3 × 5		136
Three-shuffle drill	Pause	Four per group	2 × 3		148
Crossover step	Pause	Four per group	2 × 3		149

Lifts					
Exercise	**Tempo**	**Rest**	**Sets × reps**	**Intensity**	**Page number**
Back squat	3-1-1	75 to 90	2 or 3 × 10	65, (70) 75	97
Three-way lunge	2-1-1	60	2 × 3		99
Chin-up	3-1-1	90	2 × 8 to 12		103
Single-arm, single-leg cable row	2-1-2	30	2 × 10		92
Side plank	Hold	15 to 20	3 to 5 × 15 to 20 sec.		174

THURSDAY

Plyometrics, agility, quick feet					
Exercise	**Type**	**Rest**	**Sets × reps**	**Distance**	**Page number**
Agility ladder		Team	1		142
Single-leg multidirection bound	Stick	Three per group	2		126
Backpedal intervals	Pause	Four per group	1L, 1R	10/10/10/10	149
Pivot sprint	Single	Four per group	2L, 2R	20	152
Lifts					
Exercise	**Tempo**	**Rest**	**Sets × reps**	**Intensity**	**Page number**
Hang snatch	2-0-E	90 to 120	3 × 5	75, 80, 85	114
Push-up	2-1-2	↓	2 × 8 to 12		110
Cook hip lift	Hold 5	30	2 × 5		168
Ls, Ws, Ys, and Ts	C	60	2 × 8		187
LA coordination	2-1-2	60	3 × 10 to 12		172

FRIDAY

Plyometrics, agility, quick feet					
Exercise	**Type**	**Rest**	**Sets × reps**	**Distance**	**Page number**
Half wheel hop	Pause/ cont.	Partners	2 × 1P/1C		135
Three-shuffle drill	Pause	Four per group	2 × 3		148
Crossover step	Pause	Four per group	2 × 3		149
Lifts					
Exercise	**Tempo**	**Rest**	**Sets × reps**	**Intensity**	**Page number**
Front squat	3-1-1	75 to 90	3 × 8	70, 75, 80	98
Single-leg squat	3-1-1	30	2 × 10		87
Cable row	2-1-3	60	2 × 10		106
Standing lat pull-down	2-1-3	60	2 × 10		105
Prone cobra (back)	Hold 3	60	2 × 5		180

Table 11.2 Off-Season Program: Weeks 3 and 4

MONDAY

Plyometrics, agility, quick feet					
Exercise	**Type**	**Rest**	**Sets × reps**	**Distance**	**Page number**
Agility ladder		Team	1		142
Multidirection squat and bound	Counter	Three per group	2		125
Backpedal and sprint	Pause	Four per group	4	10/10	153
Forward sprint to pivot sprint	Cont.	Four per group	2L, 2R	20/20	153
Lifts					
Exercise	**Tempo**	**Rest**	**Sets × reps**	**Intensity**	**Page number**
Jump shrug from floor	E	120	3 × 3	75, 82.5, 90	116
Single-arm, single-leg deadlift	3-1-1	30	3 × 5		89
Single-arm cable push	2-1-2	60	2 × 8		93
Front plank	Hold	30	3 or 4 × 45 to 60 sec		173
Multidirection weight plate shoulder press	1-1-1	60	2 × 5		183
Arm circle	C	60	2 × 5		189

TUESDAY

Plyometrics, agility, quick feet					
Exercise	**Type**	**Rest**	**Sets × reps**	**Distance**	**Page number**
Line hops series, single-leg variation	Cont.	Three per group	1 × 8 sec each		134
Knee tuck jump	Cont.	Four per group	2 × 8		138
Two-shuffle lateral sprint	Cont.	Four per group	2L, 2R	30	154
Lateral sprint	Pause	Four per group	2L, 2R	20/20	154
Lifts					
Exercise	**Tempo**	**Rest**	**Sets × reps**	**Intensity**	**Page number**
Back squat	3-1-1	90	3 × 8	70, 75, 80	97
Three-way lunge	2-1-1	60	2 × 3		99
Chin-up	3-1-1	90	2 × 5 to 8		103
Single-arm, single-leg cable row	2-1-2	30	3 × 8		92
Side plank with leg abduction	2-1-2	30	3 × 8		175

THURSDAY

Plyometrics, agility, quick feet					
Exercise	Type	Rest	Sets × reps	Distance	Page number
Agility ladder		Team	1		142
Single-leg multidirection bound	Counter	Three per group	2		126
Backpedal and sprint	Pause	Four per group	2 × 4	10/10	153
Forward sprint to pivot sprint	Cont.	Four per group	2L, 2R	20/20	153

Lifts					
Exercise	Tempo	Rest	Sets × reps	Intensity	Page number
Hang snatch	2-0-E	90 to 120	3 × 4	77.5, 82.5, 87.5	114
Push-up	2-1-2	↓	2 × 8 to 12		110
Bench hip extension	Hold 2	30	2 × 8		169
Ls, Ws, Ys, and Ts	C	60	2 × 8		187
LA coordination	2-1-2	60	4 × 10 to 12		172

FRIDAY

Plyometrics, agility, quick feet					
Exercise	Type	Rest	Sets × reps	Distance	Page number
Half wheel hop	Pause/cont.	Partners	2 × 1P/1C		135
Two-shuffle lateral sprint	Cont.	Four per group	2L, 2R	30	154
Lateral sprint	Pause	Four per group	2L, 2R	20/20	154

Lifts					
Exercise	Tempo	Rest	Sets × reps	Intensity	Page number
Front squat	3-1-1	75 to 90	3 × 5	75, 80, 85	98
Single-leg squat	3-1-1	No	3 × 8		87
Cable row	2-1-3	60	3 × 8		106
Standing lat pull-down	2-1-3	60	2 × 8		105
Prone cobra (back)	Hold 3	60	2 × 5		180

Table 11.3   Off-Season Program: Weeks 5 and 6

MONDAY

Plyometrics, agility, quick feet					
Exercise	Type	Rest	Sets × reps	Distance	Page number
Agility ladder		Team	1		142
Multidirection squat and bound	Cont.	Three per group	1 × 3		125
Multidirection agility (short)	Cont.	Four per group	2	8 × 5 to 6 feet	154
Lifts					
Exercise	Tempo	Rest	Sets × reps	Intensity	Page number
Jump shrug from floor	E	120	3 × 2	77.5, 85, 92.5	116
Single-leg RDL	3-1-1	60	3 × 5		90
Single-arm cable push with twist	1-1-2	60	2 × 8		111
Slide board mountain climber	C	60	3 × 8		175
Single-arm dumbbell over-the-shoulder press	1-1-1	60	2 × 8		183
Arm circle	C	60	2 × 8		189

TUESDAY

Plyometrics, agility, quick feet					
Exercise	Type	Rest	Sets × reps	Distance	Page number
Single-leg ladder hop series	Cont.	Team	2		134
Hurdle hop (single leg)	Cont.	Team	2 to 3 × 5		136
Backpedal two shuffle	Cont.	Four per group	2L, 2R	20	156
Pro agility	Cont.	Four per group	2L, 2R	15/30/15	157
Lifts					
Exercise	Tempo	Rest	Sets × reps	Intensity	Page number
Back squat	3-1-1	120	3 or 4 × 5	75, 80, 85	97
Forward and lateral lunge	2-1-1	↓	2 × 3/3		101
Chin-up	1-1-3	30	3 × 3 to 5		103
Bent row	2-1-3	60	3 × 8		108
Side bend	2-1-3	60	3 × 8		177

THURSDAY

Plyometrics, agility, quick feet					
Exercise	**Type**	**Rest**	**Sets × reps**	**Distance**	**Page number**
Agility ladder		Team	1		142
Single-leg multidirection bound	Cont.	Three per group	1 × 3		126
Multidirection agility (long)	Cont.	Four per group	1L, 1R	Half back-court	155
Lifts					
Exercise	**Tempo**	**Rest**	**Sets × reps**	**Intensity**	**Page number**
Hang snatch	2-0-E	120	3 or 4 × 3	80, 85, 90, (90)	114
Matrix reaches	C	No	2 × 3		86
Stability push-up	2-1-2	↓	8 to 12		9
Supine lateral ball roll	Hold 3	60	2 × 4		169
Ls, Ws, Ys, and Ts	C	60	2 × 8/8/8/8		187

FRIDAY

Plyometrics, agility, quick feet					
Exercise	**Type**	**Rest**	**Sets × reps**	**Distance**	**Page number**
Five-dot hop	Pause/cont.	Four per group	2 × 2P/2C		136
React forward sprint and two shuffle	Cont.	Four per group	2L, 2R	20	165
Pro agility	Cont.	Four per group	2L, 2R	15/30/15	157
Lifts					
Exercise	**Tempo**	**Rest**	**Sets × reps**	**Intensity**	**Page number**
VertiMax pause, jump, squat	Singles	90	3 × 4		119
Front squat	1-1-3	↓	5, 4, 3	75, 82.5, 90	98
Pull-up	1-1-2	90	2 × 8 to 12		103
Single-arm strap row	2-1-3	60	2 × 8 to 10		107
Three-position prone cobra	Hold 3	45 to 60	2 × 3		180

Table 11.4   Off-Season Program: Weeks 7 and 8

MONDAY

Plyometrics, agility, quick feet					
Exercise	Type	Rest	Sets × reps	Distance	Page number
Lateral hop, hop, bound	Stick	Four per group	4		128
Forward hop, hop, bound	Stick	Four per group	4		129
React forward sprint	R singles	Four per group	2	20	160
React pivot sprint	R singles	Four per group	2	20	161

Lifts					
Exercise	Tempo	Rest	Sets × reps	Intensity	Page number
Power snatch	E	120	3 × 3	80, 85, 90	115
Single-arm, single-leg deadlift	3-1-1	60	5, 4, 3		89
Single-arm cable push with twist	1-1-2	60	2 × 8		111
Slide board mountain climber	2-1-2	60	3 × 8 to 10		175
Single-arm dumbbell over-the-shoulder press	1-1-1	60	2 × 5		183
Arm circle	C	60	2 × 8		189

TUESDAY

Plyometrics, agility, quick feet					
Exercise	Type	Rest	Sets × reps	Distance	Page number
Lateral three-line agility		Three per group	2 × 8 sec		146
Depth jump	Singles	Five to eight per group	8		137
React three shuffle	R pause	Four per group	2 × 3		159
React lateral sprint	R pause	Four per group	2 × 2	15/15	160

Lifts					
Exercise	Tempo	Rest	Sets × reps	Intensity	Page number
Back squat	3-1-1	120 to 150	4 × 3	77.5, 82.5, 87.5, 90	97
Forward and lateral lunge	2-1-1	↓	2 × 3/3		101
Chin-up	1-1-3	30	2 × 8 to 12		103
Bent row	2-1-2	60	3 × 5		108
Pallof press	2-1-2	60	2 or 3 × 8		179

THURSDAY

<table>
<tr><th colspan="6">Plyometrics, agility, quick feet</th></tr>
<tr><th>Exercise</th><th>Type</th><th>Rest</th><th>Sets × reps</th><th>Distance</th><th>Page number</th></tr>
<tr><td>Forward hop, hop, lateral bound</td><td>Stick</td><td>Four per group</td><td>4</td><td></td><td>130</td></tr>
<tr><td>Back hop, hop, lateral bound</td><td>Stick</td><td>Four per group</td><td>4</td><td></td><td>131</td></tr>
<tr><td>Forward bounding lunge</td><td>Pause</td><td>Four per group</td><td>2 × 3</td><td></td><td>126</td></tr>
<tr><td>Multidirection agility (long)</td><td>R pause</td><td>Four per group</td><td>1L, 1R</td><td></td><td>155</td></tr>
<tr><th colspan="6">Lifts</th></tr>
<tr><th>Exercise</th><th>Tempo</th><th>Rest</th><th>Sets × reps</th><th>Intensity</th><th>Page number</th></tr>
<tr><td>Hang snatch</td><td>E</td><td>120</td><td>4 × 2</td><td>82.5, 87.5, 92.5, 92.5</td><td>114</td></tr>
<tr><td>Toe touch to balance</td><td>C to Q</td><td>No</td><td>1 × 5/5</td><td></td><td>84</td></tr>
<tr><td>Stability push-up</td><td>E</td><td>60</td><td>2 × 8 to 12</td><td></td><td>9</td></tr>
<tr><td>Supine lateral ball roll</td><td>Hold 3</td><td>60</td><td>2 × 5</td><td></td><td>169</td></tr>
<tr><td>Ls, Ws, Ys, and Ts</td><td>C</td><td>60</td><td>2 × 8</td><td></td><td>187</td></tr>
</table>

FRIDAY

<table>
<tr><th colspan="6">Plyometrics, agility, quick feet</th></tr>
<tr><th>Exercise</th><th>Type</th><th>Rest</th><th>Sets × reps</th><th>Distance</th><th>Page number</th></tr>
<tr><td>Agility ladder</td><td></td><td>Team</td><td>1</td><td></td><td>142</td></tr>
<tr><td>Five-dot hop</td><td>Pause/cont.</td><td>Partners</td><td>2 × 2P/2C</td><td></td><td>136</td></tr>
<tr><td>Single-plane mirror drill</td><td>Mirror</td><td>Five per group</td><td>2 lead, 2 chase</td><td></td><td>158</td></tr>
<tr><th colspan="6">Lifts</th></tr>
<tr><th>Exercise</th><th>Tempo</th><th>Rest</th><th>Sets × reps</th><th>Intensity</th><th>Page number</th></tr>
<tr><td>VertiMax jump squat singles</td><td>E</td><td>120</td><td>3 × 4</td><td></td><td>120</td></tr>
<tr><td>Box step-up</td><td>1-1-3</td><td>↓</td><td>8, 6, 5</td><td>70, 77.5, 85</td><td>102</td></tr>
<tr><td>Pull-up</td><td>E</td><td>30</td><td>2 × 5 to 8</td><td></td><td>103</td></tr>
<tr><td>Single-arm strap row</td><td>C</td><td>60</td><td>3 × 8</td><td></td><td>107</td></tr>
<tr><td>Three-position prone cobra</td><td>Hold 3</td><td>No</td><td>1 × 5</td><td></td><td>180</td></tr>
</table>

Table 11.5 Off-Season Program: Weeks 9 and 10

MONDAY

Plyometrics, agility, quick feet					
Exercise	Type	Rest	Sets × reps	Distance	Page number
Lateral hop, hop, bound	Counter	Four per group	3		128
Forward hop, hop, bound	Counter	Four per group	3		129
Medicine ball back toss	Singles	Four per group	2 × 3		124
Overhead medicine ball oblique toss	Singles	Three per group	2 × 3		185
React backpedal and sprint	R doubles	Four per group	4		163
React pivot sprint	R doubles	Four per group	4		161

Lifts					
Exercise	Tempo	Rest	Sets × reps	Intensity	Page number
Power snatch	E	120	4 × 2	82.5, 87.5, 92.5, 92.5	115
Push jerk	E	90	3 × 3	80, 85, 90	118
Single-arm cable push	1-1-2	60	2 × 5		93
Arm circle	C	60	2 × 8		189

TUESDAY

Plyometrics, agility, quick feet					
Exercise	Type	Rest	Sets × reps	Distance	Page number
Lateral three-line agility		Team	2 × 8 sec		146
Depth jump	Singles	Five to eight per group	8		137
Overhead medicine ball crunch toss	Singles	Three per group	2 × 3		185
React forward sprint and lateral sprint	R doubles	Four per group	4		162
React backpedal and lateral sprint	R doubles	Four per group	4		163

Lifts					
Exercise	Tempo	Rest	Sets × reps	Intensity	Page number
Back squat	3-1-1	90 to 120	8, 6, 4	67.5, 77.5, 87.5	97
Walking lunge with medicine ball arc	2-1-1	↓	2 × 4/4		91
Chin-up	1-1-3	30	2 × 5 to 8		103
Supine row	2-1-2	60	3 × 8 to 12		109

THURSDAY

Plyometrics, agility, quick feet					
Exercise	Type	Rest	Sets × reps	Distance	Page number
Box hop, hop, lateral bound	Pause	Four per group	2 × 3		132
Medicine ball squat push toss	Singles	Four per group	2 × 3		122
Medicine ball chop toss	Cont.	Four per group	2 × 4		184
React backpedal and three shuffle	R doubles	Four per group	4		164
React forward sprint and two shuffle	R doubles	Four per group	4		165

Lifts					
Exercise	Tempo	Rest	Sets × reps	Intensity	Page number
Hang snatch	2-0-E	120	5, 4, 3	77.5, 85, 90	114
Matrix reaches	C	No	1 × 3		86
Box plyometric push-up	E	60	2 × 5 to 8		138
Stability ball hip extension and knee flexion	2-1-2	60	2 × 5 to 8		170
Ls, Ws, Ys, and Ts	C	60	2 × 8/8/8/8		187

FRIDAY

Plyometrics, agility, quick feet					
Exercise	Type	Rest	Sets × reps	Distance	Page number
Agility ladder		Team	1		142
Box split jump	Singles	Three per group	2 × 4		133
Overhead medicine ball dribble	Cont.	Three per group	2 × 30		186
Tennis ball toss	R pause	Four per group	2 × 5		157

Lifts					
Exercise	Tempo	Rest	Sets × reps	Intensity	Page number
VertiMax continuous	E	120	3 × 5		120
Box step-up	1-1-3	↓	3 × 5	75, 80, 85	102
Pull-up	1-1-2	90	2 × 3 to 5		103
Bar rollout	3-3-2	60	2 or 3 × 8		176
Prone cobra reach and rotate	Hold 3	No	2 × 5		181

Table 11.6   Off-Season Program: Weeks 11 and 12

MONDAY

Plyometrics, agility, quick feet					
Exercise	Type	Rest	Sets × reps	Distance	Page number
Lateral hop, hop, bound	Cont.	Four per group	2 × 3		128
Forward hop, hop, bound	Cont.	Four per group	2 × 3		129
Medicine ball back toss	Cont.	Four per group	2 × 3		124
Overhead medicine ball oblique toss	Singles	Three per group	2 × 3		185
React backpedal and sprint	R doubles	Four per group	4		163
React pivot sprint	R doubles	Four per group	4		161
Lifts					
Exercise	Tempo	Rest	Sets × reps	Intensity	Page number
Power snatch	E	120	4 × 2	82.5, 87.5, 92.5, 92.5	115
Push jerk	E	90	4 × 2	82.5, 87.5, 92.5, 92.5	118
Single-arm cable push	1-1-2	60	2 × 5		93
Arm circle	C	60	2 × 8		189

TUESDAY

Plyometrics, agility, quick feet					
Exercise	Type	Rest	Sets × reps	Distance	Page number
Lateral three-line agility		Team	2 × 8 sec		146
Depth jump		Five to eight per group	8		137
Overhead medicine ball crunch toss	Singles	Three per group	2 × 3		185
React forward sprint and lateral sprint	R doubles	Four per group	4		162
React backpedal and lateral sprint	R doubles	Four per group	4		163
Lifts					
Exercise	Tempo	Rest	Sets × reps	Intensity	Page number
Back squat	3-1-1	120	5, 4, 3	75, 82.5, 90	97
Walking lunge with medicine ball arc	2-1-1	↓	2 × 4/4		91
Chin-up	1-1-3	30	3 × 3 to 5		103
Supine row	2-1-2	60	3 × 8 to 12		109

THURSDAY

Plyometrics, agility, quick feet					
Exercise	Type	Rest	Sets × reps	Distance	Page number
Box hop, hop, lateral bound	Cont.	Four per group	2 × 3		132
Medicine ball squat push toss	Singles	Four per group	2 × 3		122
Medicine ball chop toss	Cont.	Four per group	2 × 4		184
React backpedal and three shuffle	R doubles	Four per group	4		164
React forward sprint and two shuffle	R doubles	Four per group	4		165
Lifts					
Exercise	Tempo	Rest	Sets × reps	Intensity	Page number
Hang snatch	2-0-E	120	4, 3, 2	80, 87.5, 92.5	114
Toe touch to balance	C to Q	No	1 × 5/5		84
Box plyometric push-up	E	60	2 × 5 to 8		138
Stability ball hip extension and knee flexion	2-1-2	60	2 × 5 to 8		170
Ls, Ws, Ys, and Ts	C	60	2 × 8/8/8/8		187

FRIDAY

Plyometrics, agility, quick feet					
Exercise	Type	Rest	Sets × reps	Distance	Page number
Agility ladder		Team	1		142
Box split jump	Singles	Three per group	2 × 4		133
Overhead medicine ball dribble	Cont.	Three per group	2 × 30		186
Tennis ball toss	R pause	Four per group	2 × 5		157
Lifts					
Exercise	Tempo	Rest	Sets × reps	Intensity	Page number
VertiMax jump squat singles (mix)	E	120	3 × 4		120
Box step-up	1-1-3	↓	5, 4, 3	75, 82.5, 90	102
Pull-up	1-1-2	90	2 × 8 to 12		103
Bar rollout	3-3-2	60	3 × 8		176
Prone cobra reach and rotate	Hold 3	No	2 × 5		181

Table 11.7 Off-Season Conditioning

Week	Session	Drill	Set × reps	Rest	Focus	Page number
1	1	No conditioning			Recovery	—
	2	20/10	2 or 3 × 5 min (120 ft)	2 to 3 min	Conditioning base	192
2	1	20/10	3 × 5 min (120 ft)	2 to 3 min	Conditioning base	192
	2	20/10	5 min × 120 ft, 2 × 60 ft, 120 ft	2 to 3 min	Conditioning base	192
3	1	20/10	5 min × 120 ft, 2 × 60 ft, 120 ft	2 to 3 min	Conditioning base	192
	2	20/10	5 min × 120 ft, 2 × 60 ft, 4 × 30 ft	2 to 3 min	Conditioning base	192
4	1	20/10	5 min × 120 ft, 2 × 60 ft, 4 × 30 ft	2 to 3 min	Conditioning base	192
	2	1-3-1 sprint pyramid	3×	Partners, 30 sec	Conditioning base and jump introduction	194
5	1	1-4-1 sprint pyramid	2×	Partners, 60 sec	Conditioning base and jump introduction	194
	2	Jump 1-5-1 sprint pyramid	1×	Partners	Conditioning base and jump introduction	194
6	1	Jump, shuffle, jump, sprint conditioning	4 × 2	Partners, 30 to 60 sec	Increasing single-plane change of direction and jumps	194
	2	Jump 1-5-1 sprint pyramid	1×	Partners	Conditioning base	194
7	1	Jump, shuffle, jump, sprint conditioning	4 × 2	Partners, 30 to 60 sec	Increasing single-plane change of direction and jumps	194
	2	Multidirection jump	4 × 2	Partners, 60 sec	Increasing multiplane change of direction and jumps	195

Week	Session	Drill	Set × reps	Rest	Focus	Page number
8	1	Jump, shuffle, jump, sprint conditioning	2 × 4	Partners, 120 sec	Increasing single-plane change of direction and jumps	194
	2	Multidirection jump	3 × 3	Partners, 90 sec	Increasing multiplane change of direction and jumps	195
9	1	Jump, shuffle, jump, sprint conditioning	2 × 4	Partners, 120 sec	Increasing single-plane change of direction and jumps	194
	2	Multidirection jump	2 × 4	Partners, 120 sec	Increasing multiplane change of direction and jumps	195
10	1	Position threes	2 × 4	Three per group, 30 sec	Sport and position specific	196
	2	Position repetitions	4×	Three per group	Sport and position specific	197
11	1	Position threes	2 × 5	Three per group, 30 sec	Sport and position specific	196
	2	Position repetitions	2 × 3	Three per group, 60 sec	Sport and position specific	197
12	1	Position threes	3 × 4	Three per group, 30 sec	Sport and position specific	196
	2	Position repetitions	2 × 4	Three per group, 60 sec	Sport and position specific	197

Chapter 12

In-Season Programs

The in-season program is broken up into three parts: preseason (prior to competition), regular season, and postseason. The goals and formats are unique for each phase and tend to be unique to each team. It is important to note that a component of training that is implemented in the off-season should also be implemented during in-season training. To maintain the improvements achieved in the off-season, athletes must stimulate that component during in-season training. If not, performance in that component will decrease within a few weeks. For example, if agility is a point of emphasis and is trained throughout the off-season, it must remain in the protocol throughout the in-season. To maintain the adaptations gained in the off-season, however, only minimal volume is required.

PRESEASON

In most sports, the preseason lasts approximately two weeks. During this time, a four-day format with low volume (table 12.1) can be implemented to develop a base of strength. Typically, most college teams practice two or three times a day, so limiting sessions to 30 minutes or less helps combat mental and physical fatigue.

Table 12.1   Preseason Program: Weeks 1 and 2

MONDAY

Plyometrics, agility, quick feet					
Exercise	Type	Rest	Sets × reps	Distance	Page number
Agility ladder		Team	1		142
Multidirection squat and bound	Stick	Three per group	2		125

Lifts					
Exercise	Tempo	Rest	Sets × reps	Intensity	Page number
Jump shrug from floor	E	120 to 150	3 × 3	75, 82.5, 90	116
Push-up	2-1-2	60	2 × 8 to 12		110
Front plank	Hold	30	4 or 5 × 30 sec		173
Multidirection weight plate shoulder press	1-0-1	60	2 × 8		183

TUESDAY

Plyometrics, agility, quick feet					
Exercise	Type	Rest	Sets × reps	Distance	Page number
Three-shuffle drill	Pause	Four per group	2 × 3		148
Crossover step	Pause	Four per group	2 × 3		149

Lifts					
Exercise	Tempo	Rest	Sets × reps	Intensity	Page number
Back squat	3-1-1	75 to 90	2 or 3 × 8	65, (72.5), 80	97
Chin-up	1-1-2	90	2 × 8 to 12		103
Single-arm, single-leg cable row	2-1-3	60	2 × 10		92
Side plank	Hold	15	3 or 4 × 15 sec		174

THURSDAY

Plyometrics, agility, quick feet					
Exercise	Type	Rest	Sets × reps	Distance	Page number
Agility ladder		Team	1		142
Half wheel hop	Pause/ cont.	Partners	1 or 2 × 1P/1C		135

Lifts					
Exercise	**Tempo**	**Rest**	**Sets × reps**	**Intensity**	**Page number**
Hang snatch	2-0-E	120	3 × 5	75, 80, 85	114
Single-arm, single-leg RDL	3-1-1	60	2 × 5		88
Ls, Ws, Ys, and Ts	C	60	2 × 8		187
LA coordination	2-1-2	60	3 × 10 to 12		172

FRIDAY

Plyometrics, agility, quick feet					
Exercise	**Type**	**Rest**	**Sets × reps**	**Distance**	**Page number**
Backpedal intervals	Pause	Four per group	1L, 1R	10/10/10/10	149
Forward sprint to pivot sprint	Singles	Four per group	2L, 2R	20	153
Pivot sprint	Singles	Four per group	2L, 2R	20	152
Lifts					
Exercise	**Tempo**	**Rest**	**Sets × reps**	**Intensity**	
Single-leg squat	3-1-1	30 to 60	2 × 8 to 10		87
Cook hip lift	Hold 5	30 to 60	2 × 5		168
Cable row	2-1-3	60	2 × 10		106
Prone cobra (back)	Hold 3	60	2 × 5		180

IN-SEASON

The main focus of an in-season training program is on maintaining balance, strength, power, quickness, and health while promoting optimal recovery for performance in competition. Maintenance is always the goal, but many athletes I have worked with have achieved personal bests in both strength and power during the in-season. The in-season program outlined here (tables 12.2 through 12.8) is based on a Friday and Saturday competition schedule. Because of the reduced time available for training during the season, components are separated: lifting sessions are on Monday and Wednesday, and agility and plyometrics sessions are on Tuesday. In this format, the big-muscle multijoint exercises are not divided into hip and quad–dominant movements. Squats are performed at the beginning of the week to allow more recovery time before competition. Opposing pushing and pulling movements are performed together instead of on separate days in the event an athlete misses a session. This keeps balance problems between agonist and antagonist muscles from developing.

Table 12.2 In-Season Training Program: Weeks 3 and 4

MONDAY

Exercise	Tempo	Rest	Sets × reps	Intensity	Page number
Hang snatch	2-0-E	120	3 × 4	75, 82.5, 87.5	114
Back squat	3-1-1	90 to 120	8, 6, 5	65, 75, 85	97
Single-arm, single-leg cable row	2-1-2	↓	3 × 8		92
Push-up	2-1-2	60	2 × 8 to 10		110
Front plank	Hold	E	3 × 45 to 60		173
Side plank with leg abduction	2-1-2	60	2 × 8 to 10		175
Multidirection weight plate shoulder press	1-0-1	60	2 × 5		183
Arm circle	C	No	1 × 8		189

TUESDAY

Exercise	Type/Tempo	Rest	Sets × reps	Distance	Page number
Agility ladder		Team	1		142
Half wheel hop	Pause/cont.	Partners	2 × 1P/1C		135
Multidirection squat and bound	Counter	Three per group	2		125
Three-shuffle drill	Cont.	Four per group	2		148
Lateral sprint	Singles	Four per group	2	20/20	154
Backpedal and sprint	Pause	Four per group	2	10/10	153
Matrix reaches	C	No	2 × 3		86
Prone cobra (back)	Hold 3	No	1 × 8		180

WEDNESDAY

Exercise	Tempo	Rest	Sets × reps	Intensity	Page number
Jump shrug from floor	E	120 to 150	3 × 2	77.5, 85, 92.5	116
Single-leg squat	3-1-1	30	2 × 8		87
Chin-up	1-1-2	30	2 × 5 to 8		103
Bench hip extension	Hold 2	30	2 × 5 to 8		169
Ls, Ws, Ys, and Ts	C	60	2 × 8		187
LA coordination	2-1-2	60	4 × 10 to 12		172

Table 12.3 In-Season Training Program: Weeks 5 and 6

MONDAY

Exercise	Tempo	Rest	Sets × reps	Intensity	Page number
Hang snatch	2-0-E	120	3 × 3	75, 82.5, 90	114
Back squat	3-1-1	120 to 150	5, 4, 3	70, 80, 90	97
Single-arm strap row	2-1-2	↓	2 or 3 × 8		107
Push-up	2-1-2	60	2 × 8 to 10		110
Slide board mountain climber	C	E	2 × 8		175
Multidirection weight plate shoulder press	1-0-1	60	2 × 3		183
Arm circle	C	No	1 × 8		189

TUESDAY

Exercise	Type/Tempo	Rest	Sets × reps	Distance	Page number
Agility ladder		Team	1		142
Five-dot hop	Pause/cont.	Partners	1 × 2P/2C		136
Single-leg multidirection bound	Stick	Three per group	2		126
Backpedal two shuffle	Cont.	Four per group	2L, 2R	10	156
React forward sprint and pivot sprint	Cont.	Four per group	2L, 2R	20/20	162
Pro agility	Cont.	Four per group	2L, 2R	15/30/15	157
Toe touch to balance	C to Q	No	2 × 5		84
Prone cobra (back)	Hold 3	No	1 × 8		180

WEDNESDAY

Exercise	Tempo	Rest	Sets × reps	Intensity	Page number
Power snatch	E	120 to 150	3 × 3	75, 82.5, 90	115
Three-way lunge	2-1-1	↓	2 × 2		99
Chin-up	1-1-2	90	3 × 3 to 5		103
Bench hip extension	Hold 2	30	2 × 8		169
Side bend	2-1-2	30	2 × 8		177
Ls, Ws, Ys, and Ts	C	60	2 × 8		187

Table 12.4   In-Season Training Program: Weeks 7 and 8

MONDAY

Exercise	Tempo	Rest	Sets × reps	Intensity	Page number
Hang snatch	2-0-E	120	3 × 2	77.5, 85, 92.5	114
Back squat	3-1-1	120 to 150	3 × 3	70, 80, 90	97
Single-arm strap row	2-1-2	↓	2 or 3 × 8		107
Single-arm cable push	2-1-2	60	2 × 8		93
Slide board mountain climber	C	E	2 × 8		175
Single-arm dumbbell over-the-shoulder press	1-1-1	60	2 × 8		183
Arm circle	C	No	1 × 8		189

TUESDAY

Exercise	Type/tempo	Rest	Sets × reps	Distance	Page number
Agility ladder		Team	1		142
Five-dot hop	Pause/cont.	Partners	1 × 1P/1C		136
Single-leg multidirection bound	Counter	Three per group	2		126
Multidirection agility (short)	Cont.	Four per group	2		154
Multidirection agility (long)	Cont.	Four per group	1L, 1R		155
Matrix reaches	C	No	2 × 3		86
Three-position prone cobra	Hold 3	No	1 × 5		180

WEDNESDAY

Exercise	Tempo	Rest	Sets × reps	Intensity	Page number
Power snatch	E	120 to 150	3 × 3	75, 82.5, 90	115
Three-way lunge	2-1-1	↓	2 × 2		99
Chin-up	1-1-2	30	2 × 8 to 12		103
Supine lateral ball roll	Hold 3	60	2 × 4		169
Side bend	2-1-2	30	2 × 8		177
Ls, Ws, Ys, and Ts	C	60	2 × 8		187

Table 12.5   In-Season Training Program: Weeks 9 and 10

MONDAY

Exercise	Tempo	Rest	Sets × reps	Intensity	Page number
Hang snatch	2-0-E	120	3 × 5	75, 80, 85	114
Front squat	3-1-1	90	2 × 8	65, 78	98
Single-arm cable push with twist	1-1-2	↓	2 × 8		111
Bent row	2-1-2	60	2 × 8		108
Bar rollout	3-2-2	60	2 × 8		176
Single-arm dumbbell over-the-shoulder press	1-1-1	60	2 × 5		183
Arm circle	C	No	1 × 5		189

TUESDAY

Exercise	Type/tempo	Rest	Sets × reps	Distance	Page number
Lateral three-line agility		Three per group	2 × 8 sec		146
Lateral hop, hop, bound	Stick	Four per group	4		128
Forward hop, hop, bound	Stick	Four per group	4		129
React three shuffle	R pause	Five per group	2 × 2		159
React lateral sprint	R single	Five per group	2	15	160
React forward sprint	R single	Five per group	2	20	161
React pivot sprint	R single	Five per group	2	20	161
Toe touch to balance	C to Q	No	1 × 5/5		84
Three-position prone cobra	Hold 3	No	1 × 5 to 8		180

WEDNESDAY

Exercise	Tempo	Rest	Sets × reps	Intensity	Page number
Power snatch	E	120 to 150	3 × 2	77.5, 85, 92.5	115
Forward and lateral lunge	2-1-1	↓	2 × 2/2		101
Chin-up	1-1-2	30	2 × 5 to 8		103
Supine lateral ball roll	Hold 3	↓	2 × 4		169
Pallof press	2-1-2	30	2 × 8		179
Ls, Ws, Ys, and Ts	C	60	2 × 8		187

Table 12.6   In-Season Training Program: Weeks 11 and 12

MONDAY

Exercise	Tempo	Rest	Sets × reps	Intensity	Page number
Hang snatch	2-0-E	120	3 × 4	75, 82.5, 87.5	114
Push jerk	E	120	3 × 3	75, 82.5, 90	118
Front squat	3-1-1	120	3 × 5	65, 75, 85	98
Single-arm cable push	1-1-2	↓	2 or 3 × 5		93
Bent row	2-1-2	60	3 × 5		108
Bar rollout	3-2-2	60	2 × 8		176
Arm circle	C	No	1 × 5		189

TUESDAY

Exercise	Type	Rest	Sets × reps	Distance	Page number
Lateral three-line agility		Three per group	2 × 8 sec		146
Lateral hop, hop, bound	Counter	Four per group	3 or 4		128
Forward hop, hop, bound	Counter	Four per group	3 or 4		129
React backpedal and lateral sprint	R doubles	Four per group	2		163
React forward sprint and lateral sprint	R doubles	Four per group	2		162
React backpedal and sprint	R doubles	Four per group	2		163
React forward sprint and pivot sprint	R doubles	Four per group	2		162
Matrix reaches	C	No	2 × 3		86
Three-position prone cobra	Hold 3	No	1 × 5 to 8		180

WEDNESDAY

Exercise	Tempo	Rest	Sets × reps	Intensity	Page number
Power snatch	E	120 to 150	3 × 2	77.5, 85, 92.5	115
Forward and lateral lunge	2-1-1	↓	2 × 2/2		101
Chin-up	1-1-2	30	3 × 3 to 5		103
Stability ball hip extension and knee flexion	Hold 3	30	2 × 5		170
Pallof press	2-1-2	30	2 × 8		179
Ls, Ws, Ys, and Ts	C	60	2 × 8		187

Table 12.7 In-Season Training Program: Weeks 13 and 14

MONDAY

Exercise	Tempo	Rest	Sets × reps	Intensity	Page number
Overhead medicine ball crunch toss (wall)	E	Four per group	2 × 3		185
Overhead medicine ball dribble	Q	Four per group	2 × 30		186
Hang snatch	2-0-E	120	3 × 3	75, 82.5, 90	114
Push jerk	E	120	3 × 2	77.5, 85, 92.5	118
Front squat	3-1-1	120	5, 4, 3	70, 80, 90	98
Box plyometric push-up	E	↓	2 × 5 to 8		138
Supine row	1-1-3	60	2 × 8		109
Arm circle	C	No	1 × 5		189

TUESDAY

Exercise	Type	Rest	Sets × reps	Distance	Page number
Lateral three-line agility		Three per group	2 × 8 sec		146
Forward hop, hop, lateral bound	Stick	Four per group	3		130
Back hop, hop, lateral bound	Stick	Four per group	3		131
React backpedal and lateral sprint	R doubles	Four per group	2		163
React forward sprint and lateral sprint	R doubles	Four per group	2		162
React backpedal and sprint	R doubles	Four per group	2		163
React forward sprint and pivot sprint	R doubles	Four per group	2		162
Toe touch to balance	C to Q	No	1 × 5		84
Prone cobra reach and rotate	Hold 3	No	1 × 5		181

WEDNESDAY

Exercise	Tempo	Rest	Sets × reps	Intensity	
Medicine ball squat push toss	E	Four per group	2 × 2		122
Medicine ball back toss	E	Four per group	2 × 2		124

(continued)

Table 12.7 *(continued)*

WEDNESDAY *(continued)*

Exercise	Tempo	Rest	Sets × reps	Intensity	Page number
Overhead medicine ball oblique toss	E	Four per group	2 × 3		185
Medicine ball chop toss	E	Four per group	2 × 4		184
Box split jump (singles)	E	Four per group	2 × 3		133
Chin-up	1-1-2	↓	2 × 5 to 8		103
Stability ball hip extension and knee flexion	Hold 3	30	2 × 5		170
Ls, Ws, Ys, and Ts	C	60	2 × 8		187

Table 12.8   In-Season Training Program: Weeks 15 and 16

MONDAY

Exercise	Tempo	Rest	Sets × reps	Intensity	Page number
Overhead medicine ball crunch toss	E	Four per group	2 × 3		185
Overhead medicine ball dribble	Q	Four per group	2 × 30		186
Hang snatch	2-0-E	120 to 150	3 × 2	77.5, 85, 92.5	114
Front squat	3-1-1	120	3 × 3	70, 80, 90	98
Box plyometric push-up	E	↓	2 × 5 to 8		138
Supine row	1-1-3	60	2 × 8		109
Single-arm dumbbell over-the-shoulder press	1-1-1	60	2 × 5		183
Arm circle	C	No	1 × 5		189

TUESDAY

Exercise	Type	Rest	Sets × reps	Distance	Page number
Lateral three-line agility		Three per group	2 × 8 sec		146
Box hop, hop, lateral bound	Pause	Four per group	3		132
Tennis ball toss	React	Five per group	2 × 5		157
Matrix reaches	C	No	1 × 3		86
Prone cobra reach and rotate	Hold 3	No	1 × 5		181

238

WEDNESDAY

Exercise	Tempo	Rest	Sets × reps	Intensity	Page number
Medicine ball squat push toss	E	Four per group	2 × 2		122
Medicine ball back toss	E	Four per group	2 × 2		124
Overhead medicine ball oblique toss	E	Four per group	2 × 3		185
Medicine ball chop toss	E	Four per group	2 × 4		184
Box split jump (singles)	E	Four per group	2 × 3		133
Chin-up	1-1-2	↓	2 × 5 to 8		103
Stability ball hip extension and knee flexion	Hold 3	30	2 × 5		170
Ls, Ws, Ys, and Ts	C	60	2 × 8		187

POSTSEASON

Many variables affect program design in the postseason. The strength and conditioning coach should meet with the coaching staff to develop the training protocol for the postseason. Power and strength gains are usually maintained for two to three weeks after cessation of training. When considering the plan, take a realistic look at how far the team can go in the postseason (how much longer may you play for?) as well as the team's current physical state. Exercises that maintain strength and power but present a low risk for tweaks or injuries should be selected. Training volume should be very low, and rest time should be emphasized or exaggerated to promote recovery. Remember, one training session will never make an athlete, but it can definitely break her. Because of the magnitude of variables involved and the specific needs of each team, a sample postseason program is not provided.

In-season training is key to maintaining athletic performance for competition and to preventing large peaks and valleys in athletic performance throughout a year. It is important to include all training components (i.e., quick feet, plyometrics, agility, power, strength, and balance) to maximize performance. This will also help maintain or improve the progress made in the off-season.

Appendix

% 1 Rep Max Chart									
Max	92%	90%	87.5%	85%	83.5%	82%	80%	77.5%	75%
1 RM	2 RM	3 RM	4 RM	5 RM	6 RM	7 RM	8 RM	9 RM	10 RM
60	55	55	55	50	50	50	50	45	45
65	60	60	55	55	55	55	50	50	50
70	65	65	60	60	60	55	55	55	55
75	70	70	65	65	65	60	60	60	55
80	75	70	70	70	65	65	65	60	60
85	80	75	75	70	70	70	70	65	65
90	85	80	80	75	75	75	70	70	70
95	85	85	85	80	80	80	75	75	70
100	90	90	90	85	85	80	80	80	75
105	95	95	90	90	90	85	85	80	80
110	100	100	95	95	90	90	90	85	85
115	105	105	100	100	95	95	90	90	85
120	110	110	105	100	100	100	95	95	90
125	115	115	110	105	105	105	100	95	95
130	120	115	115	110	110	105	105	100	100
135	125	120	120	115	115	110	110	105	100
140	130	125	125	120	115	115	110	110	105
145	135	130	125	125	120	120	115	110	110
150	140	135	130	130	125	125	120	115	115
155	145	140	135	130	130	125	125	120	115
160	145	145	140	135	135	130	130	125	120
165	150	150	145	140	140	135	130	130	125
170	155	155	150	145	140	140	135	130	130
175	160	160	155	150	145	145	140	135	130
180	165	160	160	155	150	150	145	140	135
185	170	165	160	155	155	150	150	145	140
190	175	170	165	160	160	155	150	145	145
195	180	175	170	165	165	160	155	150	145
200	185	180	175	170	165	165	160	155	150
205	190	185	180	175	170	170	165	160	155

Max	92%	90%	87.5%	85%	83.5%	82%	80%	77.5%	75%
1 RM	2 RM	3 RM	4 RM	5 RM	6 RM	7 RM	8 RM	9 RM	10 RM
210	195	190	185	180	175	170	170	165	160
215	200	195	190	185	180	175	170	165	160
220	200	200	195	185	185	180	175	170	165
225	205	205	195	190	190	185	180	175	170
230	210	205	200	195	190	190	185	180	175
235	215	210	205	200	195	195	190	180	175
240	220	215	210	205	200	195	190	185	180
245	225	220	215	210	205	200	195	190	185
250	230	225	220	215	210	205	200	195	190
255	235	230	225	215	215	210	205	200	190
260	240	235	230	220	215	215	210	200	195
265	245	240	230	225	220	215	210	205	200
270	250	245	235	230	225	220	215	210	205
275	255	250	240	235	230	225	220	215	205
280	260	245	245	240	235	230	225	215	210
285	260	250	250	240	240	235	230	220	215
290	265	255	255	245	240	240	230	225	220
295	270	260	260	250	245	240	235	230	220
300	275	265	265	255	250	245	240	235	225
305	280	270	265	260	255	250	245	235	230
310	285	275	270	265	260	255	250	240	235
315	290	275	275	270	265	260	250	245	235
320	295	290	280	270	265	260	255	250	240
325	300	295	285	275	270	265	260	250	245
330	305	295	290	280	275	270	265	255	250
335	310	300	295	285	280	275	270	260	250
340	315	305	300	290	285	280	270	265	255
345	315	310	300	295	290	285	275	265	260
350	320	315	305	300	290	285	280	270	265
355	325	320	310	300	295	290	285	275	265

(continued)

% 1 Rep Max Chart *(continued)*

Max	92%	90%	87.5%	85%	83.5%	82%	80%	77.5%	75%
1 RM	2 RM	3 RM	4 RM	5 RM	6 RM	7 RM	8 RM	9 RM	10 RM
360	330	325	315	305	300	295	290	280	270
365	335	330	320	310	305	300	290	285	275
370	340	335	325	315	310	305	295	285	280
380	350	340	335	325	315	310	305	295	285
385	355	345	335	325	320	315	310	300	290
390	360	350	340	330	325	320	310	300	295
395	365	355	345	335	330	325	315	305	295
400	370	360	350	340	335	330	320	310	300
405	375	365	355	345	340	330	325	315	305
410	375	370	360	350	340	335	330	320	310
415	380	375	365	355	345	340	330	320	310
420	385	380	370	355	350	345	335	325	315
425	390	385	370	360	355	350	340	330	320
430	395	385	375	365	360	355	345	335	325
435	400	390	380	370	365	355	350	335	325
440	405	395	385	375	365	360	350	340	330
445	410	400	390	380	370	365	355	345	335
450	415	405	395	385	375	370	360	350	340
455	420	410	400	385	380	375	365	355	340
460	425	415	405	390	385	375	370	355	345
465	430	420	405	395	390	380	370	360	350
470	430	425	410	400	390	385	375	365	355
475	435	430	415	405	395	390	380	370	355
480	440	430	420	410	400	395	385	370	360
485	445	435	425	200	405	400	390	375	365
490	450	440	430	415	410	400	390	380	370
495	455	445	435	420	415	405	395	385	370
500	460	450	440	425	420	410	400	390	375

About the Author

Steve Oldenburg has been an assistant strength and conditioning coach for the University of Illinois since 2004. In his current position, he oversees women's volleyball, women's soccer, men's tennis, and men's golf. He has also worked with football, men's and women's basketball, women's tennis, women's golf, softball, and baseball. Collectively, his Illinois teams have won seven Big Ten titles and participated in two national championship games.

Before coming to Illinois, Oldenburg was the strength and conditioning coach for the Grand Rapids Force of the United States Professional Volleyball League (USPV).

Oldenburg is a certified strength and conditioning specialist through the National Strength and Conditioning Association. He graduated from Central Michigan University in 2001 with a bachelor of science degree in health fitness with focus on prevention and rehabilitation. Oldenburg and his family reside in Champaign, Illinois.